ASPECTS OF *KING LEAR*

OTHER 'ASPECTS' VOLUMES

ASPECTS OF
KING LEAR

ARTICLES REPRINTED FROM *SHAKESPEARE SURVEY*

EDITED BY

KENNETH MUIR

EMERITUS PROFESSOR OF ENGLISH LITERATURE
UNIVERSITY OF LIVERPOOL

AND

STANLEY WELLS

GENERAL EDITOR OF THE OXFORD SHAKESPEARE AND
HEAD OF THE SHAKESPEARE DEPARTMENT
OXFORD UNIVERSITY PRESS

CAMBRIDGE UNIVERSITY PRESS

CAMBRIDGE
LONDON   NEW YORK   NEW ROCHELLE
MELBOURNE   SYDNEY

Published by the Press Syndicate of the University of Cambridge
The Pitt Building, Trumpington Street, Cambridge CB2 IRP
32 East 57th Street, New York, NY 10022, USA
296 Beaconsfield Parade, Middle Park, Melbourne 3206, Australia

This collection first published 1982

Printed in Great Britain at the
University Press, Cambridge

Library of Congress catalogue card number: 82–4344

British Library Cataloguing in publication data
Aspects of King Lear.
1. Shakespeare, William. King Lear
I. Muir, Kenneth   II. Wells, Stanley, *1930–*
III. Shakespeare survey
822.3'3   PR2819
ISBN 0 521 24604 0 hard covers
ISBN 0 521 28813 4 paperback

UP

CONTENTS

PLATES

1 Costumes for productions of *King Lear*.

2 Costumes for productions of *King Lear*.

3 Wall painting of the Last Judgement (Guild Chapel, Stratford-upon-Avon).

4 Act I scene i: the love-trial. Marilyn Taylerson as Cordelia, Judi Dench as Regan, Barbara Leigh-Hunt as Goneril, Donald Sinden as Lear, 1976.

5 Act I scene i: 'Hence, and avoid my sight!' Lear (Eric Porter) banishes Cordelia (Diane Fletcher), 1968.

6 Act I scene iv. 'Dost thou call me fool, boy?': Eric Porter as Lear and Michael Williams as the Fool, 1968.

7 Act II scene iv. Lear kneels to Goneril (Angela Baddeley); Charles Laughton as Lear, Ian Holm as the Fool, Shakespeare Memorial Theatre 1959.

8 Act II scene iv. Paul Scofield as Lear with Goneril, 1962.

9 Act III scene ii: the storm. Charles Laughton as Lear, Ian Holm as the Fool, Shakespeare Memorial Theatre 1959.

10 Act III scene iv. 'Poor Tom's a-cold': Tony Church as Lear and Mike Gwilym as Edgar in Buzz Goodbody's production at The Other Place, 1974.

11 Act IV scene vi: ''Tis the times' plague when madmen lead the blind'. Grigori Kozintsev's film of *King Lear*, 1970, with Yuri Yarvet as Lear, K. Cebric as Gloucester and Lionard Merzin as Edgar (from *King Lear: The Space of Tragedy*, the diary of Grigori Kozintsev).

12 Act IV scene vii: 'Be your tears wet?' Louise Jameson as Cordelia and Tony Church as Lear in Buzz Goodbody's production at The Other Place, 1974.

13 Act V scene iii: 'Come, let's away to Prison. / We two alone will sing like birds i' th' cage' (from *King Lear: The Space of Tragedy*, the diary of Grigori Kozintsev).

14 Act V scene iii: 'Cordelia, Cordelia! Stay a little. Ha! / What is't thou say'st?' Yuri Yarvet as Lear and Valentina Shendrikova as Cordelia (from *King Lear: The Space of Tragedy*, the diary of Grigori Kozintsev).

All the illustrations, unless otherwise credited, are from productions at the Royal Shakespeare Theatre, Stratford-upon-Avon. Grateful thanks are due to the following for permission to reproduce their photographs: Thomas Holte (4, 6, 7); the Governors of the Royal Shakespeare Theatre, Stratford-upon-Avon (5); the Harvard Theatre Collection (8, 10); Joe Cocks (11, 13); Heinemann Educational Ltd (12, 14, 15).

PREFACE

It is arguable, as L. C. Knights has suggested, that whereas *Hamlet* was once the play which seemed to express the aspirations and frustrations of the age, now *King Lear* speaks directly to us all, whatever our beliefs or unbeliefs. Of course our view of the play is bound to be affected by our attitude to life. To Swinburne, and to numerous critics since his day, the key lines of the play are not those of choric figures such as Kent or Edgar, but Gloucester's 'As flies to wanton boys are we to the gods: / They kill us for their sport' – although, not long afterwards, and before he knows he is being succoured by Edgar, Gloucester prays directly to the 'ever-gentle gods'. A. C. Bradley, on the other hand, could argue that the theme of the play was the redemption of Lear; and his interpretation was followed by critics who would profess and call themselves Christians. John F. Danby, for example, regarded Cordelia as a Christ figure, one who redeemed 'nature from the general curse / Which twain have brought her to' – the 'twain' being Adam and Eve rather than Goneril and Regan. G. L. Bickersteth compared scenes of the play to Dante's *Purgatorio*.

There was naturally a reaction against such interpretations. Everyone noticed that the dusty answer to Albany's prayer for the safety of Lear and Cordelia was the entrance of Lear bearing the hanged Cordelia. W. R. Elton therefore argued in *King Lear and the Gods* (San Marino, California, 1966) that Shakespeare wrote a play which would not offend the pious, but containing a subtext to which sceptics and agnostics could eagerly respond. Yet in a play set in a pagan world one ought not to expect flights of angels to sing Lear and Cordelia to their rest. In any case, tragedy is bound to be pessimistic: Strindberg quite properly laughed at those people who wanted optimistic tragedies. Perhaps the most influential criticism of our time – now half a century old – is Wilson Knight's essay in *The Wheel of Fire* on the grotesque element in the play; and this has been vulgarized by some into the idea that Shakespeare was a forerunner of the Theatre of the Absurd.

The essays in the present volume cover a period of more than twenty years, mostly taken from the two volumes of *Shakespeare Survey* (13 and 33) devoted to the play. G. R. Hibbard's retrospect covers the main critical debates about the play since 1939 and the essays of Derek Peat, J. Stampfer, J. K. Walton, and Mary Lascelles show that the debate continues.

One recent trend, not otherwise represented, is touched on in Hibbard's retrospect. Until quite recently, all editors of the play, while accepting the First Folio text as the more reliable, nevertheless added the lines peculiar to the First Quarto. Now a number of critics, including Michael J. Warren, Steven Urkowitz, and Gary Taylor, have argued forcibly that the texts should not be conflated, since they believe that the Folio represents Shakespeare's own revision, its omissions and alterations being deliberate. We can never be certain, however, that all the alterations were Shakespeare's, and some of those he made may have been reluctant. It is difficult to believe that he would have cut the choric comments by Cornwall's servants at the end of Act III, when they are left alone after the blinding of Gloucester. Steven Urkowitz's book *Shakespeare's Revision of 'King Lear'* (Princeton, 1980), and Gary Taylor's essay 'The War in *King Lear*' (*Shakespeare Survey* 33), both appeared after the writing of Hibbard's retrospect, as did P. W. K. Stone's *The Textual History of 'King Lear'* (London, 1980), which argues that the quarto is based on a longhand report of the play which also strongly influenced the Folio text; but not many readers will see the necessity for the numerous emendations he proposes.

Taking their cue from Charles Lamb (who had witnessed only Tate's adaptation) many critics have declared that Shakespeare's tragedies, and *King Lear* in particular, cannot be represented on the stage. This view was authoritatively questioned by Harley Granville-Barker in his splendid *Preface*; and despite Maynard Mack's justifiable scorn of some recent performances, the period covered by this collection of essays has given the lie to Lamb's declaration. The review articles in *Shakespeare Survey* do not provide materials for a survey of productions, but we include plates illustrating some of the more important. In 1959 Glen Byam Shaw directed Charles Laughton as Lear in a pictorially pleasing version, with designs by Motley, which did not explore the text with any great profundity, though Ian Holm was a poignantly intelligent Fool. The production is described by Muriel St Clare Byrne in '*King Lear* at Stratford-upon-Avon', *Shakespeare Quarterly*, 11 (1960), 189–206. Far more in keeping with the mood of the times was Peter Brook's 1962 version (discussed in J. L. Styan's *The Shakespeare Revolution* (Cambridge, 1977), pp. 217–23), which, with Paul Scofield as the King, was regarded by many as a triumph for both director and leading actor. Brook's vision of the play was harsh and austere, not entirely sympathetic with Lear, whose knights came some way to justifying Goneril's complaints of their behaviour. Acknowledging the influence of Jan Kott, Brook observed the Folio's omission of Gloucester's consoling servants; the blinded Gloucester, a sack over his head, groped his way off the stage as the house lights rose for the interval. Scofield's performance, searching, granite-voiced, offered no opportunity for easy emotional identification. Director and actor created a climax rather in the questions of the Dover Cliff scene than in the potential resolution of the reunion of Lear and Cordelia. The play's realization, though partial, was intense. Brook's film version of 1971, with Scofield again as Lear, is sympathetically discussed in Jack J. Jorgens's *Shakespeare on Film* (Bloomington and London, 1977) along with Grigori Kozintsev's film, of 1970, which used a translation by Boris Pasternak. Kozintsev's book *King Lear: The Space of Tragedy* is the director's fascinating diary recording the film's evolution and its relationship to Kozintsev's own experience of life and art, and goes some way to explain the greatness of his film.

In Trevor Nunn's 1968 production, Eric Porter offered a less intellectual but more warmly human Lear, impressive in the egocentric grandeur of his opening scene, touchingly absurd in his divestiture on the heath, dignified in his final suffering.

Buzz Goodbody's *Lear* at The Other Place – the Royal Shakespeare Company's studio theatre – in 1974 was, as the title warned, an adaptation, shortening the play for a cast of ten, emphasizing Edmund's sexual entanglements with Goneril and Regan, demanding the audience's imaginative participation in its use of the small space, in which Tony Church's Lear and Mike Gwilym's Edgar achieved over-whelming intimacy with their audience. In 1976 Trevor Nunn, working with John Barton and Barry Kyle, again directed the play at Stratford, this time with Donald Sinden as Lear. Nunn broke away from the customary Stonehenge-type settings and costumes, as may be seen particularly in our Plate 4. There is an excellent discussion of this production in Richard David's *Shakespeare in the Theatre* (Cambridge, 1978, pp. 95–105); *Shakespeare Survey* 33 includes an interview with Donald Sinden, 'Playing King Lear'.

K.M.
S.W.W.

'KING LEAR': A RETROSPECT, 1939–79

G. R. HIBBARD

Throughout the period under review there has been a wide measure of agreement that *King Lear* is the greatest of all the plays, and, perhaps as a consequence, an equally wide measure of disagreement about what it says. In the course of the many scrutinies it has been subjected to, almost every significant word in it has been examined with minute care, as though the drama were an extended metaphysical poem; yet, paradoxically enough, there is no general consensus among editors as to what Shakespeare actually wrote; and editions differ greatly from one another in the texts they offer. G. K. Hunter, for example, in his New Penguin edition first published in 1972, lists well over a hundred readings in which his text does not concur with those of Peter Alexander (1951), Kenneth Muir (1952), and Dover Wilson and G. I. Duthie (1960).[1] The prime cause of the variations is, of course, that there are two substantive texts not one: the Quarto of 1608, containing some 300 lines not found in the Folio, and the Folio itself, containing 100 lines not found in the Quarto. The editor must, therefore, or has hitherto felt that he must, make use of both while knowing full well, to complicate his task still further, that neither of them was set up from a manuscript in Shakespeare's hand. Nevertheless, one great advance has been made. In a classic study, published in 1940,[2] W. W. Greg established conclusively that the Quarto of 1608, in a copy which, like all extant copies, was made up of both corrected and uncorrected sheets, was used for setting the Folio text. He also showed that the copy of the Quarto employed for this purpose had been collated with a text from the playhouse, in all probability the prompt-copy, and much altered in the process. His findings on this score have won general acceptance, though both G. I. Duthie, in the New Cambridge edition of the play, and G. Blakemore Evans, in the Riverside edition of Shakespeare (1974), agree with A. S. Cairncross[3] that the Folio also had some recourse to the second Quarto of 1619, a view that has been vigorously challenged and repudiated by J. K. Walton, who asserts categorically that it is 'of no value'.[4]

As well as defining the relationship between the two substantive texts, Greg's investigation also brought into sharp focus the major problem that every editor has to face, for in the course of it he discovered clear evidence 'that the folio has in some instances inadvertently reproduced errors of the quarto in place of what we must assume to have been the readings of the playhouse manuscript'. It therefore follows that 'where the folio differs from the quarto its readings...must be derived from the authoritative playhouse manuscript, whereas where the two agree we can never be certain

[1] *King Lear*, ed. G. K. Hunter (Harmondsworth, 1972), pp. 331–5.
[2] *The Variants in the First Quarto of 'King Lear'* (1940).
[3] 'The Quartos and the First Folio Text of *King Lear*', *Review of English Studies*, n.s. VI (1955), 252–8.
[4] *The Quarto Copy for the First Folio of Shakespeare* (Dublin, 1971), pp. 282–7.

that the folio has not carelessly reproduced an error of the quarto' (p. 187). Since then Charlton Hinman[1] has given editors yet another reason for treating the Folio text with some caution by demonstrating that it was not set by one compositor, B, as Alice Walker had suggested,[2] but by two, B and E, and that E, probably an apprentice and the least skilled member of Jaggard's team, was responsible for more than half of it.

In these circumstances, the nature and origin of the copy used for the 1608 Quarto has become an issue of the first importance, and has proved an extremely recalcitrant one. In 1940 Greg thought the copy had probably been obtained 'from actual performance by some method of shorthand' (p. 138). By 1955, however, he had been persuaded by G. I. Duthie[3] that shorthand was not the answer.[4] Less convinced by Duthie's theory that the copy-text was dictated to a scribe by the cast relying on their memories,[5] he found himself attracted by the freshness and ingenuity of Alice Walker's hypothesis, advanced in her *Textual Problems* (pp. 37–67), that it was derived from, as he puts it, 'a surreptitious transcript of the foul papers by two boy actors, "Goneril" dictating to "Regan", who in their haste contaminated the written text by recollections of what they were accustomed to speak and hear on the stage' (p. 382). All the same, he still had his doubts, especially about the identification of the two boys as the culprits. This last doubt was shared by Duthie, who, in his final words on a subject to which he had devoted so much of his life, accepted Miss Walker's general theory but modified it to read: 'transcription from foul papers, the persons involved having had some memorial knowledge of the play, seems the most convincing solution'.[6] J. K. Walton, however, argues that Duthie was wrong to abandon his original theory, and that memorial reconstruction still remains the likeliest answer to the question of the origin of the copy

employed by the printer of the 1608 Quarto.[7] In doing so Walton does not mention the indirect support Miss Walker's theory has received from E. A. J. Honigmann, who, pointing to the occasional greater metrical regularity of the Quarto, makes an interesting case for the idea that some of the variants between the two texts can best be explained as representing first thoughts (the Quarto) and second thoughts (the Folio) on the part of Shakespeare himself.[8] More recently still, Michael J. Warren, resorting to literary rather than bibliographical criteria, has boldly attacked the whole assumption, hitherto the basis of editorial endeavour, that there is or ever was such a thing as the ideal text of the tragedy. He holds 'that Q and F *King Lear* are sufficiently dissimilar that they should not be conflated, but should be treated as two versions of a single play, both having authority'.[9]

Greg concluded *The Variants in the First Quarto of 'King Lear'* on an optimistic and hortatory note: 'I believe that now the whole of the information needed is at the disposal of editors, and it appears to be high time that they set about the job of preparing a text of the play

[1] 'The Prentice Hand in the Tragedies of the Shakespeare First Folio: Compositor E', *Studies in Bibliography*, IX (1957); and *The Printing and Proof-Reading of the First Folio of Shakespeare* (Oxford, 1963), I, 212.

[2] *Textual Problems of the First Folio* (Cambridge, 1953), pp. 62–3.

[3] *Elizabethan Shorthand and the First Quarto of 'King Lear'* (Oxford, 1949).

[4] *The Shakespeare First Folio* (Oxford, 1955), p. 380.

[5] *King Lear*, ed. G. I. Duthie (Oxford, 1949), pp. 19–116.

[6] *King Lear*, ed. G. I. Duthie and J. Dover Wilson (Cambridge, 1960), pp. 132–5.

[7] *The Quarto Copy*, pp. 269–81.

[8] *The Stability of Shakespeare's Text* (1965), pp. 121–8.

[9] 'Quarto and Folio *King Lear* and the Interpretation of Albany and Edgar', in *Shakespeare: Pattern of Excelling Nature*, ed. David Bevington and Jay Halio (Newark, N. J., and London, 1978), p. 97.

that shall be based upon a properly reasoned estimate of the evidence' (p. 190). In 1955, when he published *The Shakespeare First Folio*, the optimism had disappeared. Summing up what had been done in the interim, which had, in fact, seen the publication of Duthie's edition of 1949, the most scholarly we have, and of Kenneth Muir's New Arden edition of 1952, the most commonly used by literary critics, he wrote: 'It is to be feared that a consideration of the various theories [about the origin of the copy for the Quarto] so far advanced can only lead to the conclusion...that *King Lear* still offers a problem for investigation' (p. 383). Nothing has been discovered since then to alter that verdict. For the editor the play remains a nightmare – and her nine-fold.

The uncertainties about the text have in no way inhibited the activity of aesthetic criticism. The last forty years have produced a formidable – one is sorely tempted to say, daunting – outpouring of studies and interpretations of the most diverse kind. The very nature of the world we live in has much to do with the interest the play excites. Shot through with hints and fears of Doomsday, *King Lear* has taken on a peculiar immediacy and urgency. It speaks to our condition. What it says varies from critic to critic for two main reasons. First, as Helen Gardner acutely observes, no one can write about *King Lear* today without, at the same time, writing about himself and 'interpreting its design in the terms of his own conception of the mystery of things';[1] and, secondly, the clear-cut conflict in it between good and evil holds out an almost irresistible invitation to ideological readings, especially in a world where Shakespeare has, to quote Harry Levin, become 'a sort of lay religion'.[2] Like the story of the Fall of the Angels, *King Lear* 'has been adopted by both parties', and has undergone, on occasions, some strange metamorphoses in the process. Paul N. Siegel, for example, improving the ending in a manner that did not

occur to Nahum Tate, assures us that Lear and Cordelia 'become reunited in eternal bliss';[3] while Jan Kott sweeps all attempts to find some positive meaning in the tragedy into the dustbins of *Endgame* thus:

In Shakespeare's play there is neither Christian heaven, nor the heaven predicted and believed in by humanists. *King Lear* makes a tragic mockery of all eschatologies; of the heaven promised on earth, and the heaven promised after death; in fact – of both Christian and secular theodicies; of cosmogony, and of the rational view of history; of the gods and natural goodness, of man made in the 'image and likeness'. In *King Lear*, both the medieval and the renaissance orders of established values disintegrate. All that remains at the end of this gigantic pantomime is the earth – empty and bleeding.[4]

Which of the two are we to accept? 'Both? one? or neither?' Confronted by Edmund's dilemma, the sensible man will, surely, opt for the last of the three possibilities, and look for guidance elsewhere.

Between these two extremes of sentimental wishful thinking and reductive nihilistic rant there is no shortage of such guidance, sometimes brilliantly illuminating, sometimes tendentiously misleading, and sometimes painfully and painstakingly moralizing and repetitious. I shall, therefore, attempt no more than to distinguish some of the main trends and major issues.

L. C. Knights, writing some twenty years ago, observed that 'the appreciation of Shakespeare, the kind of thing men have got from Shakespeare, has varied enormously at different periods'. He then went on to say:

from time to time major shifts of attention occur, and not the least significant and fruitful of these is the one that has taken place in our time, and that scholars and critics of very different kinds have helped to bring

[1] *King Lear* (1967), p. 4.
[2] *Shakespeare and the Revolution of the Times* (Oxford, 1976), p. 6.
[3] *Shakespearean Tragedy and the Elizabethan Compromise* (New York, 1957), p. 186.
[4] *Shakespeare Our Contemporary* (1964), p. 118.

about. Conceptions of the nature and function of poetic drama have been radically revised; the essential structure of the plays has been sought in the poetry rather than in the more easily extractable elements of 'plot' and 'character'.[1]

If such is indeed the case, then the new trend should be most obvious over the period in question (*c.* 1930–59) in what was written about *King Lear*, for, as Wolfgang Clemen assures us, 'An attempt to interpret a Shakespearian play solely on the basis of its imagery – a risky undertaking – would have the greatest chance of success if *King Lear* were the play in question.'[2] In fact, three years before Clemen's book came out but too late for him to make use of it, such an attempt had been made. R. B. Heilman's *This Great Stage*,[3] significantly sub-titled 'Image and Structure in *King Lear*', is based on the assertion that 'In its fullness the structure [of the play] can be set forth only by means of the patterns of imagery' (p. 32). The use of 'only' there was, not surprisingly, very strongly objected to by, among others, W. R. Keast, who condemned the work out of hand as 'in almost all respects a bad book'.[4] Yet, once the initial fuss had died down, Heilman's main findings were absorbed into the critical bloodstream with great rapidity, and have persisted there ever since. They could not be rejected because he had pointed to a feature of the play which is demonstrably there but had not been properly noticed before: the presence in it of elaborate verbal patterns made up of references to sight, smell, clothes, sex, animals, and justice, and, behind them all, the striking paradoxes of madness in reason and reason in madness. It is significant that the one serious attack on the work in more recent years, Paul J. Alpers's '*King Lear* and the Theory of the "Sight Pattern"',[5] does not deny that the sight pattern is there; instead, it argues that Heilman and those who have followed him have mistaken its import. It is also worth noting that Heilman did his work so thoroughly that little

has been added to it. William Empson examines the use of the word 'fool' in the play, but ingeniously counterpoints the approach through 'pattern' with an approach through 'character' in order to bring out the different results they can give;[6] and Rosalie Colie puts some of Heilman's discoveries into a larger historical context in the chapter on *King Lear* in her *Paradoxia Epidemica*,[7] where she relates the paradoxes in the tragedy to the Renaissance tradition of paradox in general, and shows how they are closely interwoven with one another, much as his patterns are.

Yet, exciting and important as Heilman's book was and remains, it did little to alter existing judgements on the play's larger significances, though it did add an extra dimension to one's sense of Shakespeare's artistry in conveying them. His final conclusions about what *King Lear* says do not differ greatly from Bradley's. In revealing what a close study of the imagery could accomplish he had also, unintentionally, revealed what it could not. At this point I turn to Knights's own essay on the play. Its main contention is that *King Lear* is 'timeless and universal'.[8] It makes good this claim by concentrating, as D. A. Traversi had done,[9] on the conflict within the mind of the hero as the core of the tragedy, the focus from which everything else radiates. It is true that Knights uses the poetry to illustrate the points he makes; but the strength of the essay lies in its psychological penetration and imaginative grasp. In fact, the approach is,

---

[1] *Some Shakespearean Themes* (1959), pp. 13–14.
[2] *The Development of Shakespeare's Imagery* (1951), p. 133.
[3] Baton Rouge, 1948.
[4] 'Imagery and Meaning in the Interpretation of *King Lear*', *Modern Philology*, 47 (1949), 45.
[5] *In Defense of Reading*, ed. Reuben A. Brower and Richard Poirier (New York, 1962).
[6] *The Structure of Complex Words* (1951), pp. 125–57.
[7] Princeton, 1966.
[8] *Some Shakespearean Themes*, p. 84.
[9] '*King Lear*', *Scrutiny*, XIX (1952–3).

in no small measure, traditional. By 1959, when *Some Shakespearean Themes* appeared, the idea that the 'poetry' alone could provide the master-key to understanding was losing its hold.

In the same essay Knights says that *King Lear* 'marks a moment of great importance in the changing consciousness of the civilization to which it belongs', and then proceeds to a short consideration of the way in which the connotations of the word 'Nature' were undergoing a radical shift at the time when the play was written. Here he is taking up a topic which had interested him for a long time and which had already affected the criticism of *King Lear*. He touches on it in 'How Many Children had Lady Macbeth?' (1933), where he links it to the idea of order; and the economic and social crisis of the early seventeenth century is very much to the fore in his *Drama and Society in the Age of Jonson* (1937). Somewhere at the back of it all lie the influence of R. H. Tawney, the preoccupation of the thirties and forties in England with social change, and the developing study, especially in the United States, of the history of ideas. The impact of the last on the interpretation of *King Lear* is evident in Theodore Spencer's treatment of the play, where much emphasis falls on microcosm and macrocosm: the connexions between family, state, and the gods.[1] Combining this kind of interest with a wide knowledge of medieval and sixteenth-century drama, S. L. Bethell distinguishes two meanings of 'Nature' in the tragedy: 'first, nature as opposed to supernature, or the realm of grace; and secondly, nature as opposed to civilisation' (p. 56). The second nature is, he suggests, incarnate in Edmund, who represents the 'new thought' of Machiavelli, while supernature appears as Cordelia, who is 'associated with theological terminology and Christian symbol' (p. 59).[2] A similar kind of thinking, at the political level, is present in Edwin Muir's *The Politics of 'King Lear'*, which envisages the action as a dramatization of the destruction of the Middle Ages by a gang of Renaissance adventurers.[3] The final step towards giving *King Lear* a significant place in the history of ideas and of social change was taken by John Danby in his *Shakespeare's Doctrine of Nature: A Study of 'King Lear'*.[4] In it he contends that the good characters in the play see Nature, much as Hooker saw it, as God-ordained, benignant, and ordered; while the bad characters see it as Machiavelli had done, and as Hobbes was soon to do. The action thus becomes a struggle between the Middle Ages and the Renaissance, and, more than that, between two forms of society: 'Edmund's is the society of the New Man and the New Age...Lear's is the feudal state in decomposition' (p. 138). Above and beyond both stands Cordelia, representing the ideal: 'Nature in its communal aspect'.

Making a good deal of play with traditions of Christian communism, this was an attractive thesis at the time when it appeared, particularly in an England where there was a strong feeling that 'distribution should undo excess,/And each man have enough', and it won many adherents. Since then it has come under fire from Robert Ornstein, who accuses Danby of oversimplifying and oversubtilizing Shakespeare's intention because 'the attempt to define Goneril, Regan, and Edmund ideologically merely diverts attention from the true philosophical drama of the play which is focused in Lear's mind'.[5] Nevertheless, the main thesis has continued to exert a strong appeal. It has been adopted by Nicholas Brooke and Maynard Mack, among others, while

[1] *Shakespeare and the Nature of Man* (New York, 1942).
[2] *Shakespeare and the Popular Dramatic Tradition* (1944).
[3] Glasgow, 1947.
[4] 1949.
[5] *The Moral Vision of Jacobean Tragedy* (Madison and Milwaukee, 1960; paperback edn 1965), p. 264.

Rosalie Colie has carried its social implications a stage further by seeking to relate some aspects of the play to the crisis of the aristocracy described by Lawrence Stone.[1] Its capacity to endure would seem to indicate that it was something more than a *King Lear* for the forties.

As well as bringing out the clash between the two ideas of Nature in the drama, Danby tries, much more questionably, to turn Shakespeare himself into a medieval poet, whose work can best be interpreted by medieval methods of exegesis. He writes of Cordelia: 'she is a figure comparable with that of Griselde or Beatrice: literally a woman; allegorically the root of individual and social sanity; tropologically Charity "that suffereth long and is kind"; anagogically the redemptive principle itself' (p. 125). Here his argument links up with and becomes part of the most important development of the forties: a strong trend towards making *King Lear* an explicitly Christian tragedy. Two tendencies, which might, on first sight, appear antagonistic, came together to assist in the process. On the one hand, there was, among some of Bradley's followers, an impulse to free some of his more hesitant insights from the cautions and reservations with which he had so carefully hedged them in; on the other, there was the growing reaction against his heavy reliance on character study, and the attempt to replace it by an approach through theme, imagery, and symbol, such as that which Wilson Knight had already employed, with fresh and illuminating results, in his *The Wheel of Fire*, where, incidentally, he says that Cordelia 'represents the principle of love' (p. 201).

In *Shakespearean Tragedy* Bradley tentatively suggests that *King Lear* might not unfittingly be called *The Redemption of King Lear*. He does this, startlingly and paradoxically enough, within the overall framework of his conviction that Shakespearean tragedy is secular, that any theological interpretation of the world by the author is excluded from it, and that the play, 'the most terrible picture that Shakespeare painted of the world', does not contain 'a revelation of righteous omnipotence or heavenly harmony, or even a promise of the reconciliation of mystery and justice'. Nevertheless, his alternative title is, he thinks, justified because the King's sufferings have the effect of 'reviving the greatness and eliciting the sweetness of [his] nature', and "the gods", who inflict these sufferings on him, do so in order to enable him to attain 'the very end and aim of life'. The Christian implications of that final remark are, despite Bradley's calculated retention of 'the gods', inescapable. The statement is inconsistent with everything he says at the end of his first chapter on the play; but the temptation it held out to others, especially when coupled with the word 'redemption', was too strong to be resisted.

Combining Bradley's alternative title with another of his more adventurous suggestions, to the effect that the tragedy, in its concern with the ultimate power in the universe, affects the imagination as the *Divine Comedy* does, though the two works are entirely different in kind, R. W. Chambers came to see *King Lear* as 'a vast poem on the victory of true love', moving from the *Purgatorio* to the *Paradiso*, where 'Lear, consoled, ends by teaching patience to Gloucester and to Cordelia'.[2] He was followed, in his optimistic reading, by S. L. Bethell, who views the world of the play as one without revelation but seeking for some sort of moral and religious order, which is symbolized by Cordelia, who is constantly associated with Christian doctrine;[3] by G. L. Bickersteth, for whom Cordelia is the symbol

[1] 'Reason and Need: *King Lear* and the "Crisis" of the Aristocracy', in *Some Facets of 'King Lear': Essays in Prismatic Criticism*, ed. Rosalie L. Colie and F. T. Flahiff (Toronto and Buffalo, 1974).

[2] *King Lear* (Glasgow, 1940), pp. 48–9.

[3] *Shakespeare and the Popular Dramatic Tradition*, pp. 54, 60.

of divine love in a pagan setting;[1] and, of course, by John Danby. All of them agree that Lear becomes a better man for his sufferings, and that the tragedy is, to quote J. C. Maxwell, 'a Christian play about a pagan world'.[2] The wide currency this view gained is evident from the prominence given to it in Kenneth Muir's introduction to his New Arden edition (1952).

Even in the forties, however, at least two powerful voices were raised in opposition. F. P. Wilson stated emphatically: 'No compensatory heaven is offered. Man has only himself and his own power and endurance to fall back on. These are very great, but when they fail only madness or death remains, and death is, if not nescience, escape into the unknown.'[3] George Orwell, characteristically going his own independent way, not only denied that the play is Christian but also disposed briskly of the idea that Lear is regenerated. The old King dies, he tells us, 'still cursing, still understanding nothing', having failed to recognize that 'If you live for others, you must live *for others*, and not as a roundabout way of getting an advantage for yourself', this being the true meaning of 'renunciation', which is, as Orwell sees it, what the play is really about.[4] In the early fifties more voices joined these two. Convinced that the tragic experience is not compatible 'with any form of religious belief that assumes the existence of a personal and kindly God' (p. 18), Clifford Leech contends that the comedy in *King Lear* helps us to accept the play's picture of life 'because it confirms our most private judgment, our deepest awareness of human folly' (p. 82);[5] and William Empson, also much preoccupied with folly, inclines to Orwell's view that the King does not become wise, and retorts to those who think he becomes patient: 'if Lear really seemed regenerated to the point of accepting his calamities (including the death of Cordelia) the play would become sickly'.[6]

A more sustained and damaging attack came from D. G. James, gathering weight from having behind it one of the most wide-ranging considerations of the play as a contribution to man's knowledge of himself in his world that the entire period has to offer. *The Dream of Learning*[7] is based on the idea that 'poetry... issues from a peculiar labour of knowing' (p. 78), different from but no less important than the labour that goes into scientific knowing, an idea that James attempts to establish by bringing together *Hamlet*, *The Advancement of Learning*, and *King Lear*. So far as the last is concerned, James contends that the drive of the play is an effort to penetrate to the limits of human experience. Consequently, while there are 'signs that Christian belief was moving in Shakespeare's mind in the course of its composition' (p. 119), 'what seems certain is that it was [his] fully conscious decision not to give the story any fraction of a Christian context. The play's action is terrible in all conscience; but there is no crumb of Christian comfort in it' (pp. 92–3). All the same, Lear emerges from his madness a changed man; and the tragedy makes its own non-doctrinal affirmation, because the good characters continue to act out of wholly disinterested motives right to the end. This conclusion is not dissimilar to that reached by Arthur Sewell, following a different route, in his *Character and Society in Shakespeare*.[8] Affirming that 'the Christian-allegorical interpretations recently placed upon certain of Shakespeare's works (especially *King Lear* and *The Winter's Tale*) are almost certainly in error' (p. 60), and rejecting outright Danby's identifi-

[1] *The Golden World of 'King Lear'* (1946).

[2] 'The Technique of Invocation in *King Lear*', *Modern Language Review*, 45 (1950).

[3] *Elizabethan and Jacobean* (Oxford, 1945), p. 121.

[4] 'Lear, Tolstoy and the Fool', *Shooting an Elephant* (1945).

[5] *Shakespeare's Tragedies and Other Studies in Seventeenth-Century Drama* (1950).

[6] *The Structure of Complex Words*, p. 154.

[7] Oxford, 1951.

[8] Oxford, 1951.

cation of Cordelia with Charity, Sewell finds that the distinctive feature of *King Lear* is that 'the characters are imagined not only as members of each other but also as members of a nature which is active both within themselves and throughout the circumambient universe. Man is nowhere so certainly exhibited as a member of all organic creation and of the elemental powers' (p. 117).

It is against this background, to which, by the time Barbara Everett wrote, Paul N. Siegel had added his thoroughgoing Christian version of the drama,[1] that one must set her astringent article 'The New *King Lear*'.[2] In it, making no mention of such allies as Orwell, James, and Sewell, she attacks what she calls the orthodox approach to the play, focusing her attention mainly on Muir's introduction to his edition, which she finds fault with for its excessive, as she sees it, emphasis on the Christian content of the drama at the expense of everything else. This is not strictly true, for one of the most valuable features of that introduction is its extensive treatment of the play's sources. This said, however, there is no denying that the essay is acute and very much to the point. It accuses the Christian allegorizers of attaching more importance to the 'poetry' than to the plot; of overlooking Bradley's honest doubts about his own transcendental reading of the ending; and, most importantly, of reducing the specific concerns of the play to a rather platitudinous moralizing, a charge that Keast had levelled at Heilman some ten years before. What matters is, she contends, less what Lear learns than that it is Lear, royal Lear with his demand for absolutes, who learns it, and learns it in a peculiarly direct and physical manner.

The article does not stand alone. The year in which it came out, 1960, also saw the appearance of other writings which move in the same general direction as it does. Robert Ornstein, too, rejected moralizing, saying rather neatly: 'One can of course read *Lear* as a warning against pride, wrath, or relatives. But I suspect that like all great tragedy *Lear* actually celebrates the vulnerability of man, the sublime folly of his "needs" and aspirations, the irrationality of his demands upon the vast inscrutable universe which surrounds him' (p. 273).[3] Two powerful and well reasoned essays in *Shakespeare Survey 13* took issue with Bradley's reading of the play's ending. J. Stampfer, noting that Lear's illusion that Cordelia lives is not confined to his last speech but recurs several times after he enters carrying her body, decides, in his 'The Catharsis of *King Lear*', that the tension in the King right up to the moment of his death is 'between an absolute knowledge that Cordelia is dead, and an absolute inability to accept it' (p. 2). J. K. Walton takes another road to a similar destination. The main experience of Lear in the latter half of the play is, he argues, a continuous enlargement of consciousness. So for him to believe, to the very end, that his daughter is still alive reverses 'the direction of the whole movement which has been taking place' (p. 17). Bradley is, therefore, wrong about 'Lear's Last Speech', as the essay is entitled. To these witnesses one must also add Maynard Mack, who, in his richly suggestive article 'The Jacobean Shakespeare',[4] writes of Lear at the end of the play:

the man before us...who sweeps Kent aside, rakes all who have helped him with grapeshot...exults in the revenge he has exacted for Cordelia's death, and dies self-deceived in the thought she still lives – this man is one of the most profoundly human figures ever created in a play; but he is not, certainly, the Platonic ideal laid up in heaven, or in critical schemes, of regenerate man. (p. 38)

[1] *Shakespearean Tragedy and the Elizabethan Compromise.*
[2] *Critical Quarterly*, 2 (1960).
[3] *The Moral Vision of Jacobean Tragedy.*
[4] *Jacobean Theatre*, ed. J. R. Brown and B. Harris (1960).

Looking back from the vantage-point of today, one can see, I think, that a crucial shift was taking place round about 1960, not only in the controversy as to whether *King Lear* is, or is not a Christian tragedy, but also in critical assumptions and methods. But the shift took time. Two works appearing in that year reassert the Christian reading in all its fullness. G. I. Duthie, in his introduction to the New Cambridge edition, says the play is 'about education...conversion, spiritual regeneration, the attainment of salvation' (p. xx); sees Cordelia and Kent as Christ-like figures; and finds a just and merciful, though, he feels constrained to add, inscrutable, God behind the entire action. Irving Ribner is no less assured. Combining his extensive knowledge of medieval and sixteenth-century drama with an almost indiscriminate resort to symbolism – 'All the characters perform symbolic functions' – in the chapter on the play in his *Patterns in Shakespearian Tragedy*,[1] he has no hesitation about saying that *King Lear* 'affirms justice in the world, which it sees as a harmonious system ruled by a benevolent God' (p. 117).

Few critics and scholars since then have gone quite so far as that, though many continue, as well they might, to see the Lear of the latter part of the play as a better man than the Lear of the first two acts. Chief among the few are Virgil K. Whitaker[2] and Roy W. Battenhouse.[3] Assuming that *King Lear* rests on 'the Christian concept that God permits suffering to try and refine the natures of men' (p. 210), Whitaker, unwittingly one trusts, reveals some of the grislier implications of that notion by telling us, for example, that Lear 'has been stretched long enough upon the rack of this tough world, not so much because he can endure no more as because he has become patient and resigned, perfected in the "ripeness" that is all. He is a higher kind of man for the stretching' (p. 227). Even the blinding of Gloucester is seen simply as an appropriate punishment for the lustful

man (p. 237). The fact that it is more immediately and more pressingly the ironical consequence of Gloucester's charity and heroism in helping the old King his master is conveniently overlooked. Battenhouse goes to work after another fashion. Calling typology to his aid, and taking it for granted that both Shakespeare and his audience were as well versed in the teachings of St Augustine as he is himself, he finds the play informed by 'a background sense of parable, which...turns about the possibilities for human progress under providence' (p. 301). There is immense learning behind the book, but one cannot but conclude that it has been misapplied.

Oddly enough Battenhouse makes no more than a passing reference to William Elton's *'King Lear' and the Gods* (1966),[4] which had come out three years before his own work, and in which the whole question of whether the play is an optimistically Christian drama receives the most thorough and scholarly examination it has ever been subjected to. Looking at the tragedy in the light of the religious beliefs, disbeliefs, and disputes of the time when it was written, Elton distinguishes four main attitudes towards the ultimate governance of the world and the operation of providence in it that are to be found in both Sidney's *Arcadia* and Shakespeare's play. They are: *prisca theologia*, the position of the virtuous heathens who were on the way, as it were, to Christian thinking; atheism; superstition; and *Deus absconditus*, the notion of an inscrutable providence. Having identified these positions, Elton equates the characters of the play with them. Cordelia and Edgar exemplify the first; Goneril, Regan, and Edmund, the second; Gloucester, the third; and Lear himself, the fourth. It all looks highly

[1] 1960.
[2] *The Mirror up to Nature* (San Marino, 1965).
[3] *Shakespearean Tragedy: Its Art and Its Christian Premises* (Bloomington and London, 1969).
[4] San Marino.

schematic, yet it does throw an enormous amount of fresh light on the question it attempts to answer. Elton's principal conclusions are: that it is to underestimate 'the complexity both of the play and of Lear's character' to say that he 'repents and attains humility and patience, thus becoming fit for heaven' (p. 283); that 'the double plot is an instrument of complexity, the assurance of a multifaceted ambivalence which, contrary to the salvation hypothesis, probes and tests, without finally resolving, its argument of mysterious human suffering' (*ibid.*); and that the play as a whole is best described as 'a syncretically pagan tragedy' (p. 338). Since those words were written, Robert G. Hunter has tackled the same problem by putting *King Lear* alongside the tragedies which have an undeniably Christian background – *Richard III*, *Hamlet*, *Othello*, and *Macbeth* – a procedure which leads him to the view that in *King Lear* 'Shakespeare dramatizes the final possibility: there is no God'.[1]

That verdict too will no doubt be contested, but in its seeming finality it sounds a suitable note on which to leave this particular topic. Before doing so, however, I must record two reflections which the story of this long-drawn-out controversy brings with it. On the one hand, the determination with which believers and unbelievers alike seek to annex (if that is not too strong a word) the tragedy to their cause is a tremendous tribute to its power and significance; on the other, the peripheral nature, as it seems to me, of much of the learning brought to bear on the issue suggests that there is a real danger that criticism of *King Lear* may degenerate into an arid kind of scholasticism.

Fortunately, that danger has been recognized by some students of the play for some time. The new direction which critical thinking begins to take around 1960, less concerned with ideological considerations and dwelling more on the poignantly human experience that *King Lear* embodies, becomes clear not only in Knights's essay but also in John Holloway's treatment of the tragedy in his *The Story of the Night* (1961).[2] In it he expresses his dissatisfaction with the view that the ending is an affirmation of the value of love, because the word 'love' is too vague to cope with 'the range, power and variety of the issues of life on which this incomparable work has touched'; what matters most is that Cordelia is not content to love, she seeks to do – to recover her father his right. This anticipates, in some ways, Paul J. Alpers's dismissal of the whole tendency to make Cordelia a symbolic figure, of which he says: 'Cordelia is Cordelia. Surely there is no need to identify her with the abstraction Love in order to say that she is extraordinarily loving.'[3] Moreover, he will have no truck with the kind of moralizing which, he asserts, falsifies the essential experience. He writes:

If we treat Lear's recognition of Cordelia as a moral awareness that gives him a new personal identity, we must claim that his suffering is a good. It seems to me that we must say that Lear's suffering is shocking and heartbreaking and also (not 'and yet') it enables him to say 'Thou art a soul in bliss' and then to recognize his daughter. (*Ibid.*)

This is the kind of response that leads on naturally to Nicholas Brooke's wonderfully economical and penetrating analysis of the drama in his *Shakespeare: King Lear*.[4] Working his way through the play as it unfolds, he finds the pattern of the action to be one in which hope after hope is raised only to be dashed, a process which reaches its culmination in Albany's speech about rewards and punishments, which is abruptly broken off and made

[1] *Shakespeare and the Mystery of God's Judgments* (Athens, Georgia, 1976).
[2] London.
[3] '*King Lear* and the Theory of the "Sight Pattern"', p. 152.
[4] 1963.

totally irrelevant by Lear's last speech.[1] Questioning the idea that a sense of 'affirmation' is the proper response to tragedy, and thus, by implication, the desire for 'affirmation' which led Bradley to the notion of redemption, Brooke sums up his final impression in these words: 'all moral structures, whether of natural order or Christian redemption, are invalidated by the naked fact of experience' (pp. 59–60). Within the context of his book, this appears as something he was led to, not something he hoped to find, still less set out to find.

Maynard Mack's '*King Lear' in Our Time*,[2] though it sums up much that had gone before in an admirably lucid and readable manner, seems rather muted by comparison with his incisive and direct response to the play's ending in 'The Jacobean Shakespeare', too cluttered by references to the homiletic tradition; but we are back on what seems to me to be the high-road of more recent criticism with Helen Gardner's close-packed lecture on the tragedy,[3] where, in a very brief space, she does justice to its 'extraordinary unity of action, character-ization, and language' by saying something significant about each without, I think, using the word 'symbol' at all. It is a far cry from this searching and elegant piece of condensa-tion to Marvin Rosenberg's *The Masks of King Lear*,[4] which is anything but elegant. Never-theless, the determination to approach the play without preconceptions as to what it means informs this work also. Rosenberg's concern is with *King Lear* not merely in the study or the classroom but in the theatre and the film studio also. As he painstakingly makes his way through the text scene by scene, almost line by line at times, considering one interpretation after another, one begins to ask what can come out of such a procedure, in which all witness seems to be equally valid. Is not this to trust the player rather than the play? The answer is a firm no. His report on what he finds is both convincing and helpful because he has done the necessary work before making it. After challenging one's ready-made responses on issue after issue, he writes: 'The dark, deadly, grimly comic world of *Lear* evokes so wide and intense a range of responses on so many levels of consciousness...that it must defeat any attempts to enclose its meaning in limited formulae such as redemption, retribution, end-game, morality, etc.' (p. 328).

The same distrust of formulas is evident in H. A. Mason's analysis of *King Lear* in his *Shakespeare's Tragedies of Love*[5] and in the writings of several more recent critics. Mason is astringent and stimulating in the way that Empson can be, especially in his questioning of the play's artistry. At other times he seems simply wrong-headed, as when he blames Gloucester for not intervening in I, i, where the decisive action takes place while Gloucester is off stage. But one cannot help but applaud the firmness with which he insists that in the middle of the play Gloucester 'rises in stature to a major figure' (p. 207) and the vigour with which he asserts, in his final sentence: 'Lear dies an obstinately unreconstructed rebel' (p. 226). A similar sense of the old King's heroic quality makes itself felt in Arthur G. Davis's *The Royalty of Lear*,[6] and in S. L. Goldberg's *An Essay on 'King Lear'*,[7] though in each case one is left wondering whether the essay proper might not have served the author's purpose better than the book.

The contributions of philosophers and of critics with strong philosophical leanings, such

[1] This matter is pursued further and expanded by John D. Rosenberg in his 'King Lear and His Comforters', *Essays in Criticism*, XVI (1966), and by John Shaw in his '*King Lear:* The Final Lines', *ibid.*

[2] Berkeley, Los Angeles, and London, 1965.

[3] *King Lear.*

[4] Berkeley, Los Angeles, and London, 1972.

[5] 1970.

[6] New York, 1974.

[7] Cambridge, 1974.

as Stanley Cavell[1] and Walter Stein,[2] to the understanding of *King Lear* will, one hopes, continue; and Emrys Jones's brilliant exposition of the play's structure in his *Scenic Form in Shakespeare*[3] deserves far more than a passing mention. So does much else. But, like time, that takes survey of all the world, this piece, that takes survey of forty years, must have a stop.

[1] 'The Avoidance of Love: A Reading of *King Lear*', in his *Must We Mean What We Say?* (New York, 1969).

[2] *Criticism as Dialogue* (Cambridge, 1969).

[3] Oxford, 1971.

SOME ASPECTS OF THE STYLE OF
KING LEAR

BY

WINIFRED M. T. NOWOTTNY

Perhaps one reason why *King Lear* has been mistaken for an unactable play is that it is so nearly an unreadable play: taken passage by passage, it is so flat and grey that the better one knows it the more one feels on reopening its pages that this is almost (as Byron said of *Caractacus*) 'a tragedy complete in all but words'; the style alone might lead one to suppose that what happens in *King Lear* happens in some realm of the imagination beyond ear and eye. This cannot be true, but how is the difficulty of the language to be resolved? The apocalyptic sublime in Lear's defiance of the storm, however much it sticks in the memory, is not the play's climax, nor does this style continue. What of the rest? The 'simplicity' of the closing scenes has been remarked, as has the effective contrast with Lear's former pretensions, but in remarking this we tend to look through the language to what it is 'about', commending it only for transparency and truth to nature, and though we know that such scenes are not to be had by taking a tape-recorder to a deathbed, the terms in which to discuss this style have eluded us. It has been suggested that its art is to be discerned by tracing thematic patterns that give density or bite, but this explanation is vitiated by the fact that other plays by Shakespeare are said to have it too; the case has not been argued that the absence from *Lear* of resplendent imagery, idiosyncrasy of mind expressed in mannered style, indeed of poetry that survives quotation out of context, is deliberately compensated for by an unusually high charge of thematic power. Moreover the suggestion that the play's language draws its power from a sustained thematic undercurrent conflicts with one's obscure sense that what is really peculiar about the language is the freedom and unexpectedness of its melodic line; Lear himself is unfailingly astonishing, and this property of his words is resistant to explanation in terms of the recurrence of patterns, though, perhaps, in order to maintain this astonishment without having the play fall to bits, Shakespeare might find himself compelled to labour in the vocabulary towards the minimum number and maximum generality of moral and philosophical concepts. For, indeed, the first peculiarity of the style is that its originality is not discernible from its vocabulary, which lays a ground of permanent moral values either instantly identifiable or else so wide as to take their specific colour only from the usage of each speaker; the cultural diversity reflected in the vocabulary of *Hamlet* would be, by the standards of *Lear*, as 'finical' as Oswald seems to Kent; the deeply emotive vocabulary of *Macbeth* or the iridescence of physical and affective experience in *Othello* could have done nothing but obscure, in *Lear*, the terror of a universe whose few simple pillars fall ruining. In this respect *Lear* is at the opposite extreme from that play with which its subject has closest connection, *Timon*; the particularity of detail there, the supple periodicity of syntax sustaining a diction far removed from stereotypes of evaluation, is so much unlike the language of *Lear* that to study the rampant inventiveness of the *Timon* style opens one's eyes wider to the magnitude of the stylistic mystery in *King Lear*. What Timon says of his changed fortunes,

Shakespeare might have said of the change that came over his language between the writing of these two plays:

> myself,
> Who had the world as my confectionary,
> The mouths, the tongues, the eyes and hearts of men
> At duty, more than I could frame employment,
> That numberless upon me stuck as leaves
> Do on the oak, have with one winter's brush
> Fell from their boughs and left me open, bare
> For every storm that blows: I, to bear this,
> That never knew but better, is some burden.

What then in the language of *Lear* compensates for its apparent limitations?

First, there is less need for imagery than in other Shakespearian tragedies. Evaluating imagery that projects the conflict or quality of the hero (such as the Pontic sea and the perfect chrysolite images in *Othello*, or the cosmic, heraldic and mythological imagery used for Antony) is unnecessary where the hero is physically the image of his own tragedy. Coleridge observed that Lear has no character and does not need one because old age is itself a character and this peculiarity in the play's subject is repeated at the level of imagery. Lear is visibly old and helpless and later is visibly destitute and mad. The play, to concentrate large issues, need only advert to what the stage has given: 'a head so old and white as this'...'these white flakes'... 'Was this a face / To be opposed against the warring winds...to watch—poor perdu! — / With this thin helm?' On these terms, even a stage direction is tragic language: '*Enter Lear with Cordelia in his armes.*' The consciousness of this art may be judged by the frequency with which the play resorts to sights recognized as eloquent by the characters who see them, and by Shakespeare's care to point out their significance. There are, however, two very remarkable images of Lear's sufferings: the vulture at the heart and the wheel of fire. Both are aimed at conveying intensity rather than the structure of an experience or the quality of a man; both speak of what cannot be seen, yet is powerfully asserted to be going on here and now in the body: 'she hath tied Sharp-tooth'd unkindness, like a vulture, *here*'; 'Thou art a soul in bliss; but I am bound / Upon a wheel of fire, *that mine own tears / Do scald* like molten lead'. In both, as also in the less vivid image of 'the tempest in my mind', the body is tied to what tortures (in the tempest image, the 'greater malady' is 'fix'd'). The quality of this writing can best be discussed by way of comparisons. If we put beside it Hamlet's 'I have that within which passeth show', it becomes clear that Lear's language makes the same point whilst avoiding any appearance of concern with the 'show'. If we put beside it Gloucester's 'I am tied to the stake and I must stand the course' it becomes clear that Lear's language is not merely analogical; Lear's images of torture are embedded in sentences that bind the suffering body of the speaker to the instrument of his torture and so manage the two terms (what tortures, and what feels) as to achieve maximum impact of the cruelty of the one on the sensitivity of the other: consider simply the placing of the terms in 'a vulture, here' and the contrast between 'a wheel of fire' and 'mine own tears' (again syntactically contiguous); consider too the reality of a wheel that is brought in to explain why the tears are hot (the word 'that' is used here to mean 'and that is why' or 'in that'). If we put beside these the image used by Kent, 'he hates him much / That would upon the rack of this tough world / Stretch him out longer', it is clear that the common idea of the incommensurateness of the suffering body to what it has to endure is conveyed not so much by citing the vulture, the wheel or the rack as by making the incommensurateness a reality (rather than an analogical way of speaking). Moreover Kent's image is deployed in a sentence shaped for no other purpose than to support the analogy, whereas Lear's images of wheel and vulture seem to erupt from sentences that did not foreknow their ferocity. I labour here under the heavy difficulty of seeking to retrace in language those swift judgements that our common linguistic habits lead us to make without conscious reflection, and I would not attempt so peculiar a task were it not that I think the power of Lear's language is to be located at a level as hard to see, and as inevitably operative, as this. Since it is not to be believed that the play's power operates independently of the art of dramatic language, and since none the less this language is resistant to familiar critical tools, one must examine the possibility that its impact is due not to its displayed deviations from the language of common life but to its exploitation of the common responses we cannot avoid making when confronted by expressively ordered language. One way of breaking through to this level of power in language is to find methods for seeing the apparently simple and inevitable locution as a willed structure of functioning parts. Comparison is one method. Another is substitution for, or disordering of, the parts; when the light of the original language goes out, one knows one has broken the circuit, and where. I am encouraged to believe that so far I am on the right track because comparison has thrown up results that relate themselves to my impression that what is effective in Lear's language is its free line, the apparent absence of contrivance in the sudden blazes that illuminate the prosy syntax and commonplace vocabulary of Lear's utterances. I am the more encouraged in that these comparisons, though drawn from the main stratum of the play (the presentation of what it is to suffer), show a difference between the language of Lear and that of other characters treating the same topic. Lear's domination of the play is a linguistic domination; his is the most powerful of the voices that speak out of sufferings. Shakespeare concentrates upon Lear the style that gives a felt experience of the incommensurateness of human nature to what it must endure. In the encounter with Poor Tom, as in the poetic images, the contrasted terms are again in contiguity: '...to answer with thy *uncovered body this extremity of the skies.*' The syntactical manipulation does not obtrude its art but the art can be judged of by setting alongside this a passage from *Timon* which handles the same topic with a fuller battery of terms but without Lear's 'simple' force: Call the creatures

> Whose naked natures live in all the spite
> Of wreakful heaven, whose bare unhoused trunks,
> To the conflicting elements exposed,
> Answer mere nature.

Moreover, this passage, when put alongside that other passage in *Lear* to which its subject closely relates it—

> Poor naked wretches, wheresoe'er you are,
> That bide the pelting of this pitiless storm,
> How shall your houseless heads and unfed sides,
> Your loop'd and window'd raggedness, defend you
> From seasons such as these?

—is equally inferior in the placing of its terms. In Lear's way of saying these things, what sounds like a natural prose order is in fact more effective than the periodic syntax of Apemantus and though one might have expected the latter to afford more scope for telling juxtaposition of contrasted terms, in fact it is in the 'natural' syntax that the more powerful effect is engineered. (If a man who had already written 'bide the pelting' and 'how shall...raggedness defend you' and 'answer with thy uncovered body this extremity', *afterwards* set to and wrote 'unhoused trunks, / To the conflicting elements exposed, / Answer...', then we should all go away and eat our critical hats or beat them into coxcombs.)

It is of importance in Shakespeare's design that Lear's language though carrying all this power should appear to be uncontrived and matter-of-fact. Gloucester may strain language to express what he conceives—

thy fierce sister

In his anointed flesh stick boarish fangs.
The sea, with such a storm as his bare head
In hell-black night endured, would have buoy'd up,
And quench'd the stelled fires

—or Albany call Goneril fiend, devil and monster, or Lear himself use even more violent language in the cursing episodes, but for Lear's actual prolonged bearing of a suffering to which he is tied, vociferation is useless. A similar contrast obtains between Gloucester's language in the blinding scene and the style in which he speaks in his blind wanderings; a simplicity is invented for Gloucester which does not trench upon the simple mode of Lear, but is compatible enough with it to make their encounter linguistically possible. The play is deeply concerned with the inadequacy of language to do justice to feeling or to afford any handhold against abysses of iniquity and suffering. Gloucester's denunciation, 'I shall see / The winged vengeance overtake such children' is savagely nullified by 'See't shalt thou never...Upon these eyes of thine I'll set my foot'. *Lear* begins where *Timon* ends, that is with a vision of the futility of language to encompass or direct reality: 'Lips, let sour words go by and language end.' And fittingly, when Lear enters with the body of Cordelia, his demand for lamentation is not a demand for words—'Howl, howl, howl.' One of the things this play has to say about feeling and suffering is that they are beyond words. This poses the basic problem of the play's dramatic language.

The first steps towards dealing with this problem are taken in the action, characterization and substance of the dialogue rather than in the language itself. The opening scene makes it abundantly clear that the deepest feelings do not run out into words. Next, the glib and free-thinking Bastard expresses in soliloquy his rejection of the meanings others attach to words and public forms, and goes on to show how he can manipulate them to betray. In the third scene Goneril is displayed rigging the showdown with Lear; the fourth shows Kent planning to 'defuse' his speech, but reiterates the characterization of him as 'blunt' and 'plain'; we then meet the Fool, giving a pyrotechnic display of the half-riddling form of expression peculiarly his own. Lear is now surrounded by a collection of characters in whom the relation of meaning to verbal expression is in some way defective, oblique or trumped-up. The master-stroke of the quarrel scene with Regan and Goneril is their indifference to all the verbal forms Lear grasps at to fix the chaos of his emotions or to appeal to their supposed better natures. The master-stroke of Lear as outcast was to surround him with characters whose meanings are overlaid by or filtered through some mesh that makes communication indirect—and then to make Lear seek among the utterances of these and among the burning recollections of his experiences of the false Regan and Goneril and the misunderstood Cordelia for clues in the effort to understand the nature of things and find a form of response. At the heart of Lear's tragedy there lies the great problem of traditional symbolic forms. These are the only language for love and reverence; they have, however, to be maintained against attack, and the function of authority is to enforce observance of form on those who repudiate it. The play begins by breaking from above and from below the cultural pattern that gives shape to the flux of life. From above, Authority takes the tragic step of asking for a token of love, beyond that reverence for the forms of duty it knows itself able to enforce, whilst at the same time abrogating its power: 'Since now we will divest us, both of rule, / Interest of territory, cares of state—/ Which of you shall we say doth love us most?' From below, the Bastard, following in Gloucester's footsteps ('she...had, indeed, sir, a son for her cradle ere she had a husband for her bed') rejects reverence for forms ('Wherefore should I / Stand in the plague of custom...') and acts on his rejection. This double break opens the play's central action: the anatomy of uncontrolled evil and the anatomy of formless feeling. It is, I believe, from some such point of view that one can best appreciate the linguistic art of the play, and the way in which the minor characters are used to support the language of its hero, who must use language not as the adequate register of his experience, but as evidence that his experience is beyond language's scope.

If the problem is seen in these terms, a technique of *montage* seems the obvious solution. Shakespeare 'mounts' (and of course places) a passage in such a way that its depth of meaningfulness is *inferred* from something not strictly contained within that passage itself. This technique is sustained variously: by contrasts, by preparatory passages (especially those indicating a turmoil of feeling vaster than any one expression of any one of its forms), and by surprise. Some instances of it have already had their due in criticism, as for instance the way in which Lear's 'I did her wrong', striking through the Fool's prattle, indicates feeling running deep under the surface of the dialogue; again, the use of the Fool, harping on the prudent course, to suggest the larger dimensions of Lear's concerns. The technique, however, is continuous throughout. The Fool fills in the pauses in which Lear casts about for suitable reaction to what confronts him; what Lear finally says then comes as almost an epigram for the unspoken turmoil, as in

> *Goneril.*   ...do you that offence,
>   Which else were shame, that then necessity
>   Will call discreet proceeding.
> *Fool.*   For, you know, nuncle,
>   The hedge-sparrow fed the cuckoo so long,
>   That it had it head bit off by it young.
>   So, out went the candle, and we were left darkling.
> *Lear.* Are you our daughter?

The bluntness of Kent, if it had no other function in the play, would have been worth inventing for the sake of Lear's reactions to it in the scene of the stocks; Kent's reiteration of the brutal truth fights stubbornly with Lear's refusal to admit and face what it must mean, and the tension of the contradictions tells us that Lear's incredulity is a dam over which the chaotic flood of feeling will have to break:

> *Lear.* What's he that hath so much thy place mistook
>   To set thee here?
> *Kent.*   It is both he and she;
>   Your son and daughter.
> *Lear.* No.
> *Kent.* Yes.
> *Lear.* No, I say.
> *Kent.* I say, yea.
> *Lear.* No, no, they would not.
> *Kent.* Yes, they have.

When the dam breaks, it is with 'They durst not do't; / They could not, would not do't; 'tis worse than murder'. It is because so much is at stake that Lear has pitted himself against Kent's bluntness so long, and these exchanges intensify the meaning of the naturalistic speech in which Lear's turmoil of discrete responses breaks out, showing that the attitudes he brings to Regan's behaviour are compounded of the remnants of autocracy ('durst not'), of an appalled sense of what it implies ('could not'), and a pathetic need for and belief in Regan ('would not'), which itself is part self-deception, as the long struggle to force a fair construction upon Regan's demeanour in the ensuing scene so clearly shows. This turmoil is followed by characteristic overstatement, ''tis worse than murder', and then, as soon as the outrage has been faced, by a characteristic attempt to deal with it by the assumption of kingly dignity, reflected in the sudden recovery of the regularity of the rhythm, in the antithetical 'which way / Thou mightst deserve, or they impose', and in the climax 'Coming from us'. Upon the basis of this preparation is mounted the quarrel scene, which is great not by virtue of projecting into heightened language some one strain of emotion, but by tracing through shifts of diction and rhythm the Protean forms Lear's hurt casts up and the tragic failure of all of them to stay fixed or to make any difference to those he tries to reach through them. Is there anywhere in literature a comparable attempt to make us understand from within the one unadmitted compulsion, the need for love, that makes its victim box the compass of attitudes with such rapidity and apparent inconsistency? The language that carries this depends, for effect, on our responding as we do to language heard in ordinary life but—because it is after all the language of art—the cues for response are writ large. And further, we are in advance put upon interpreting it properly by the 'naturalistic' dialogue between Lear and Gloucester that precedes Regan's entry. Upon Gloucester's 'You know the fiery quality of the duke', Lear bursts out 'Vengeance! plague! death! confusion! Fiery? what quality?' He is not disputing the fact of the Duke's temper (as in the Quarto's botch, 'what fierie quality'); he is dismissing his right to have any temper at all that could concern a King, let alone a fiery one, and his next words are meant to call Gloucester to his senses ('Why, Gloucester, Gloucester') and to stress what is due to Lear by using titles sarcastically, 'I'ld speak with the *Duke* of Cornwall and *his wife*'. Gloucester's unhappy reply so incenses Lear (by its implication that he must wait the pleasure of his betters) that he flies at its terms—'Inform'd them! Dost thou understand me, man?' and then with

icy displeasure anatomizes the situation: 'The king would speak with Cornwall; the dear father /
Would with his daughter speak', and uses (in the Folio text) for each bond of duty the appropriate verb: 'commands, tends service' (commands it from a subject, expects it of a daughter)
and he goes on to substitute for 'fiery' the contemptuous 'hot': 'the fiery duke? Tell the hot
duke that—'. In these exchanges Lear reacts to and uses language as it is used in common life;
his attitudes are expressed not in an overtly heightened theatrical language but through the
implications, expressive choices, and significant usages available in the common tongue. But
Shakespeare writes into this common speech pointers to what prompts it. For instance, the
abrupt shift to a resolutely different attitude is cued by the unfinished state of 'Tell the hot
duke that—' and by the explicit 'No, but not yet'; the forced nature of this attempted tolerance
is brought out by the contrast between its suddenly regular rhythm and syntax, and the exclama-
tory irregularity of the preceding lines. Then this forced calm breaks in the middle of a line,
to the accompaniment of wrenched accent: 'To take the indisposed and sickly fit / For the sound
man. Death on my state! wherefore / Should he sit here?' This style exploits the expressive
ranges of common language (cueing it where necessary) and supports the expressiveness by
metrical mimesis; it is a style far removed from 'poetic' blank verse that uses the conventional
licence of poetry to elaborate a literary equivalent of the state of feeling supposed in the speaker,
yet we must admit this style to be, in its own way, far removed from the 'naturalism' that
seems merely to transcribe common speech. And though this is by no means the only style
used in the play, it is one that makes it easy to overlook the art, and to suppose the play to be
deficient in heightened language. Upon these exchanges with Kent and Gloucester Shakespeare
mounts the great quarrel scene that follows, where Lear's turmoil of conflicting attitudes is
conveyed through the obliquities, the expressive choices and nuances and even the extravagances
and transparent pretences of language as used by the common man making a scene. But we
should not forget how much is done to support this language; especially, that the very shifts
of tone illuminate one another by contrast, and that the whole scene would have been impossible
if Lear's hopes of Regan, set off against his despair of Goneril, did not so clearly annotate his
ambivalence to both; it was not for nothing that Shakespeare contrived in the plot to get
Goneril to Regan's house.

This 'mounting' of great passages on verbal encounters that prepare for them (and even,
ultimately, on characterization and plot) is a continuous technique, and to bear it in mind may
make some apparent miracles of style less impregnable to commentary. When Lear wakens in
the presence of Cordelia and says, 'You do me wrong to take me out of the grave', though no
critical words are needed to draw attention to the astonishing effect of this, it would need a spate
of words to trace the cause, but leaving aside considerations of diction, prosody and syllabity,
one may observe that what matters very much is that this is precisely the most unexpected
thing Lear could have said; it is mounted on the immediate background of Cordelia's prayerful
concern and pity, her anxiety for 'restoration' and 'medicine', her sense of the wrong others
have done him. This is why Lear astonishes us—but astonishment is as swiftly subsumed into
understanding when these words are revealed to be Lear's interpretation of what he sees, an
interpretation at once morally true and factually 'still, still, far wide': 'Thou art a soul in bliss;
but I am bound / Upon a wheel of fire, that mine own tears / Do scald.' Indeed, throughout this
scene, the language taken line by line or speech by speech resists attempts to trace effect to

cause, for each reverberates against the others, whilst at the same time being itself epigrammatic of vast issues in the antecedent action; the language, despite its simplicity of diction, is sculptural and lapidary in effect. Yet this is none the less a linguistic feat: what moves us is written into the language. One cause of our responses I cannot particularize except by some such term as 'contrast in dimension' (as between, for instance, 'wheel of fire' and 'tears'). A contrast of dimension has already characterized the language in which Lear explored man's bondage to sufferings of infinite depth, and this contrast now re-enters the language with augmented force. Just before the reunion scene opens, Gloucester makes explicit the tragic triad of sensitivity, vast sorrows, and protracted endurance: 'how stiff is my vile sense, / That I stand up, and have ingenious feeling / Of my huge sorrows!' The language of the reunion scene reiterates the contrast (as in 'this great breach in his abused nature', in 'those violent harms' and in the speech 'Was this a face / To be opposed?') but the scene goes beyond the play's earlier point of view by adding a further dimension, that of the holiness of the human being. 'Abused nature' is commended to the cure of kind gods and then, by a further rapid contrast, to the cure of little human pieties; 'let this kiss / Repair those violent harms'. In Cordelia's great speech of retrospect and pity the diction charges the poor human body with dignity ('these white flakes') as it charges the elements with majesty ('the deep dread-bolted thunder') yet at the same time, it reiterates, now under the aegis of pity, the diminutiveness of man's warfare ('this thin helm'...'fain, poor father, to hovel thee'). In this very element of holy compassion, Lear, wakening, burns anew.

A test of the relevance of such suggestions as I have made, is whether they throw light on the language which in the last scene conveys that truth to nature all recognize it to have. '*Enter Lear with Cordelia in his armes*': visual language reaches sublimity here, putting all the play has said into one visible word and bringing the whole plot to its point. Along the receding planes keyed into this tableau we see in an instant of time Lear's sin and its retribution, the wider evil that has struck both, the full fatherhood of Lear bearing his child in his arms whilst at the same time the natural course of life is seen reversed (Lear senile, so lately cared for by Cordelia), the world's destruction of the love and forgiveness that had transcended it—for the reverberation of the reunion is still strong and the language of that scene has opened the way to those suggestions of a saviour's death which now make it inescapable that Cordelia dead in her father's arms and displayed by him to the world, should strike deeply into responses that lie midway between religion and art. 'Howl, howl, howl': there is to be no language for meanings such as these; the point is reiterated in '*Had* I your tongues and eyes, I'd use them so / That heaven's vault should crack' and with the descent to 'She's gone for ever!' it is as though Shakespeare announced that the language to come is not heaven-shattering uproar, but the terms of common grief. And perhaps the greatest single reason why such terms become uncommon language is the prosody. Its function is obvious, once one looks; but who does, at such moments? Yet we shall not estimate this language rightly if we ignore it. This almost miraculous prosodic art defeats conjecture as to how far it was consciously contrived or how far it sprang with the certainty of long expertise subserving the fury of creation. Lear's 'Howl', iterated (according to the Folio) thrice, rises clear above the metrical pattern into a diapason that leaves the prosodic norm, as it leaves vocabulary, far below, obliterated. Yet still the ear, never losing the expectation of the iambic pentameter, hears this diapason as cut short, abandoned (contrast 'No, no, no, *no*! Come, let's away to prison'); the missing arsis of the second foot is so palpable that the Globe editors filled it in. Shakespeare has managed the apparently impossible feat of making a dumb ululation of terrible length seem inadequate. In the next line the norm is restated with perfect regularity. In the following line the extrametrical final syllable of 'ever' exemplifies the fitness with which in this play Shakespeare uses this licence. It is used in general, as is the frequent mid-line ending of Lear's speeches, to make Lear's own rhythm swing free of conformity to expected pattern, but in the execution of this general effect there is a notably successful placing of these freedoms so that they support the sense of the words. Such prosody adds decisively to the expressiveness of the diction; indeed it is as though Shakespeare filled up the blank verse pattern not from what our mere vocabulary offers but from the intonation patterns of expressive English speech. In the line 'Corde | lia, | Corde | lia! Stay | a litt | le. Ha!' the name is pronounced differently the second time. This is exactly what we all do in calling a name again after getting no answer. One can hear the increasing urgency expressing itself in changed intonation and stress. How Shakespeare came to do all this does not matter, but by doing it he wrote the interpretation of the words into the blank verse structure. Lear's 'Never, never, never, never, never!', a recognized stroke of prosodic art, is not isolated; it is the masterstroke of a prosodic brilliance that helps to make the play's language transcend that natural language of human feeling which it so convincingly simulates.

And, as to my final suggestion that a 'contrast of dimension' is a characteristic of the play's tragic vision: surely it hardly needs saying that the heartbreak of the very last scene is in the contrast between infinite concern and the finiteness of its object; put into words, it is all hope and all despair divided by the down of a feather: 'This feather stirs: she lives! if it be so, / It is a chance which does redeem all sorrows / That ever I have felt.'

MADNESS IN *KING LEAR*

BY

KENNETH MUIR

Shakespeare has many portraits of madness, real and assumed, and he returned to the theme again and again. Dr Pinch tries to exorcise Antipholus of Ephesus; Titus Andronicus is driven mad by his sufferings; Feste, disguised as Sir Topaz, pretends to exorcise Malvolio; Hamlet, unbalanced as he is, feigns madness, and Ophelia is driven mad by grief; Constance is driven distracted by her loss of Arthur; Portia, and perhaps Lady Macbeth, commit suicide while of unsound mind; and in *The Tempest* the three men of sin are maddened by the workings of conscience, so that their brains are as useless as a tumour.[1] It says much for Shakespeare's powers of observation or for his intuitive understanding of the human mind that his depiction of madness, though based no doubt on sixteenth-century theory, has satisfied medical opinion of later ages. J. C. Bucknill in his *Remarks on the Medical Knowledge of Shakespeare*[2] (1860) and H. Somerville in *Madness in Shakespearian Tragedy*[3] (1929) illustrate the fact that our increasing knowledge of madness during the past century has served only to justify Shakespeare's intuitions. Ella Freeman Sharpe, indeed, was so impressed by the depiction of Lear's madness that in her *Collected Papers on Psycho-Analysis* (1950) she argued that the play reflected the traumatic experiences of Shakespeare himself and that 'psychically he regressed to the loves and hates of early childhood', re-enacting his infantile desire not to share his mother's love either with her husband or with other children.[4] This theory is worth referring to, not because it is anything but wildly improbable, but because it shows that the madness depicted in the play has not been rendered false by the passage of time.

We may assume that the relation of the poet to his work is different from that posited by Ella Freeman Sharpe. The greater the artist, Eliot assures us, the wider the gulf between the heart that suffers and the mind that creates. But we may agree with D. G. James who argued that

Lear was contained in the Shakespeare who gave him birth; his passions, and the passions of the other characters, were felt and realized in Shakespeare who suffered in them. Therefore, the idea of *King Lear* we have is also the life of Shakespeare as he was then; and in contemplating the play we become what we behold; as he was what he created.[5]

There is no madness in the old play of *King Leir*, none in the story of Lear as told by Holinshed, Spenser, in *The Mirror for Magistrates*, or in any other version before Shakespeare's time, and none in Sidney's story of the Paphlagonian King. If the madness was suggested by the contemporary story of Brian Annesley[6] and his three daughters—the older ones being harsh, and the youngest, Cordell, kind—we may be sure that it was not merely the desire for topicality that made Shakespeare take the suggestion as a cat laps milk. Maeterlinck believed[7] that Shakespeare deliberately unsettled the reason of his protagonists, and thus opened

the dike that held captive the swollen lyrical flood. Henceforward, he speaks freely by their mouths; and beauty invades the stage without fearing lest it be told that it is out of place.

Orwell, on the other hand, regarded[8] Lear's madness as a protective device to enable Shakespeare to utter dangerous thoughts. Shakespeare, he says, is

noticeably cautious, not to say cowardly, in his manner of uttering unpopular opinions. Almost never does he put a subversive or sceptical remark into the mouth of a character likely to be identified with himself. Throughout his plays the acute social critics, the people who are not taken in by accepted fallacies, are buffoons, villains, lunatics or persons who are shamming insanity or are in a state of violent hysteria. *Lear* is a play in which this tendency is particularly well marked. It contains a great deal of veiled social criticism...but it is all uttered by the Fool, by Edgar when he is pretending to be mad, or by Lear during his bouts of madness. In his sane moments Lear hardly ever makes an intelligent remark. And yet the very fact that Shakespeare had to use these subterfuges shows how widely his thoughts ranged.

Against Maeterlinck's view it must be objected that the mad scenes of *King Lear* are no more lyrical than the rest of the play; and against Orwell's view of Shakespeare as the subversive sceptic without the courage of his own convictions it must be pointed out that none of his characters should be taken as his own mouthpiece. Ulysses' views on Order are shared by Rosencrantz, whom Shakespeare treats with scant sympathy, and considerably modified by the King in *All's Well that Ends Well*.[9] We cannot even be certain that the *Sonnets* are autobiographical. We cannot tell whether Shakespeare was a cowardly sceptic or a natural conformist. His acceptance of the 'establishment' and his criticism of it are equally in character. This is not to say that no point of view emerges from each play and from the canon as a whole; but the point of view is complex, subsuming both the anarchical and the conformist. The Shakespearian dialectic is not a reflection of the poet's timidity but of his negative capability.

   In the dialogue with Gloucester in IV, vi, Lear's invective has a double target—the hypocrisy of the simpering dame and the hypocrisy of the law. There is no evidence to show that Shakespeare was sheltering behind a mask. The attack on lechery can be paralleled in the diatribes of Timon and the attack on authority and law is no more extreme than that of the eminently sane Isabella or that of the praying Claudius who knew that

> In the corrupted currents of this world
> Offence's gilded hand may shove by justice,
> And oft 'tis seen the wicked prize itself
> Buys out the law.

Lest the audience should be tempted to dismiss what Lear says as mere raving, Shakespeare provides a choric comment through the mouth of Edgar:

> O, matter and impertinency mix'd!
> Reason in madness!

Lear's mad speeches, moreover, are all linked with other passages in the play. The revulsion against sex, besides being a well-known symptom of certain forms of madness,[10] is linked with Lear's earlier suspicion that the mother of Goneril and Regan must be an adultress,[11] with Gloucester's pleasant vices which led to the birth of Edmund and ultimately to his own blinding, and to Edmund's intrigues with Goneril and Regan. The attack on the imperfect instruments of justice, themselves guilty of the sins they condemn in others, is merely a reinforcement of Lear's speech in the storm, before he crossed the borders of madness:

> Let the great gods,
> That keep this dreadful pother o'er our heads,
> Find out their enemies now. Tremble, thou wretch,
> That hast within thee undivulged crimes,
> Unwhipp'd of justice: hide thee, thou bloody hand;
> Thou perjur'd, and thou simular man of virtue
> That art incestuous: caitiff, to pieces shake,
> That under covert and convenient seeming
> Hast practis'd on man's life: close pent-up guilts,
> Rive your concealing continents, and cry
> These dreadful summoners grace.[12]

Here, as in the mad scene, the justice of the gods, from whom no secrets are hid, is contrasted with the imperfections of earthly justice.

One of Lear's first speeches after his wits begin to turn consists of a prayer to 'houseless poverty':

> Poor naked wretches, wheresoe'er you are,
> That bide the pelting of this pitiless storm,
> How shall your houseless heads and unfed sides,
> Your loop'd and window'd raggedness, defend you
> From seasons such as these? O, I have ta'en
> Too little care of this! Take physic, pomp;
> Expose thyself to feel what wretches feel,
> That thou mayst shake the superflux to them,
> And show the heavens more just.[13]

It has not escaped notice that Gloucester expresses similar sentiments when he hands his purse to Poor Tom:

> heavens, deal so still!
> Let the superfluous and lust-dieted man,
> That slaves your ordinance, that will not see
> Because he does not feel, feel your power quickly;
> So distribution should undo excess,
> And each man have enough.

This repetition is of some importance since Schücking has argued[14] that it is not really consistent with Shakespeare's philosophy to see in the play a gradual purification of Lear's character. Shakespeare, he argues, nowhere associates compassion for the poor 'with a higher moral standpoint'. The point is not whether Lear's pity was intended to arouse the audience's sympathy for him, nor even whether Shakespeare himself agreed with Lear's sentiments, but whether the audience would understand that his newly aroused concern for the poor was a sign of moral improvement. Here, surely, there can be no doubt. Shakespeare's audience was not so cut off from the Christian tradition as not to know that charity was a virtue; and the fact that similar sentiments are put into Gloucester's mouth is a reinforcement of Lear's words. If Lear were mad at this point—and he has not yet crossed the frontier—he would be expressing reason in madness. Even Schücking is constrained to admit that Lear's later criticisms of society show profound insight; but he claims that this does not exhibit a development of Lear's character, because it is dependent on a state of mental derangement. The Lear who welcomes prison with Cordelia

is not a purified Lear from whose character the flame of unhappiness has burnt away the ignoble dross, but a nature completely transformed, whose extraordinary vital forces are extinguished, or about to be extinguished.

But, as I have pointed out elsewhere,[15] the three moments in the play crucial to Bradley's theory of Lear's development—his recognition of error, his compassion for the poor, and his kneeling to Cordelia—occur either before or after his madness; and Schücking seems insufficiently aware of the 'reason in madness' theme so essential to the play's meaning.

Shakespeare was only following tradition in making fool and madman the vehicle of unpopular truths;[16] and Lear's Fool disappears from the play at the moment when his master, as madman, can carry on the Fool's role. But whereas the Fool's criticism is mostly directed against Lear himself, Lear's is directed against the hypocrisies and injustices of society.

It is sometimes asserted that Shakespeare and Webster were the only two dramatists of the period to treat madness as other than matter for mirth. But, in fact, Kyd's portraits of Isabella and Hieronimo, and especially the anonymous Painter scene in *The Spanish Tragedy*, are quite serious in intention; and though the mad scene in *The Honest Whore*, Part I, may have aroused some laughter, as indeed the mad scenes in *King Lear* may have done, Dekker was careful to prepare the way for a more sympathetic reaction on the part of the audience. Anselmo remarks:

> And tho twould greeue a soule, to see Gods image
> So blemisht and defac'd, yet do they act
> Such anticke and such pretty lunacies,
> That spite of sorrow they will make you smile.[17]

Later in the scene the First Madman rebukes the visitors for their laughter:

Do you laugh at Gods creatures? Do you mock old age you roagues? is this gray beard and head counterfet, that you cry ha ha ha?

But neither Kyd nor Dekker, nor even Webster, use their madmen for any fundamental criticism of society. Bucknill was right when he pointed out that Lear's madness releases his imagination.

It is only when all the barriers of conventional restraint are broken down, that the native and naked force of the soul displays itself. The display arises from the absence of restraint, and not from the stimulus of disease.[18]

Joseph Warton and others have argued that Lear was virtually mad when he divided his kingdom; but the steps of his descent into madness are clearly marked by Shakespeare. When Kent, after Cordelia has been banished, tells the King:

> be Kent unmannerly,
> When Lear is mad...

it is obvious that Kent does not regard his master as insane; and when Regan and Goneril discuss their father at the end of the scene, they complain that his age is full of changes, that he has shown poor judgement, that even in his prime 'he hath ever but slenderly known himself'; and that they must

look to receive from his age, not alone the imperfections of long-engraffed condition, but therewithal the unruly waywardness that infirm and choleric years bring with them.

The evil daughters accuse him of the approach of senility, but not of madness.

Lear is driven insane by a series of shocks. First, there is the attack by Goneril (I, iv). This makes him angrily pretend not to know her, or to know himself, but at this point it is still pretence:

> Doth any here know me? This is not Lear:
> Doth Lear walk thus? speak thus? Where are his eyes?
> Either his notion weakens, or his discernings
> Are lethargied.—Ha! waking? 'Tis not so.—
> Who is it that can tell me who I am?

Later in the same scene he begins to realize that he has wronged Cordelia:

> O most small fault,
> How ugly didst thou in Cordelia show!...
> O Lear, Lear, Lear!
> Beat at this gate, that let thy folly in,
> And thy dear judgement out!

In the next scene he comes to a full recognition of his folly: 'I did her wrong.' All the Fool's remarks in both scenes are designed, not to distract Lear's attention from Goneril's ingratitude, but to remind him of his foolishness in dividing his kingdom and banishing Cordelia. It is arguable that the Fool's loyalty to Cordelia helps to drive his master mad. At the end of the Act Lear has his first serious premonition of insanity:

> O, let me not be mad, not mad, sweet heaven!
> Keep me in temper: I would not be mad!

The second great shock comes in the second act when Lear finds Kent in the stocks. This causes the first physical symptoms of hysteria, which were probably borrowed by Shakespeare from Harsnett's pamphlet on demoniacs or from Edward Jorden's *Brief Discourse of a Disease Called the Suffocation of the Mother* (1603), which shows 'that divers strange actions and passions of the body of man, which in the common opinion, are imputed to the devil, have their true naturall causes, and do accompanie this Disease'. But the symptoms would now be described as 'racing heart' and 'rising blood pressure':

> O, how this mother swells up toward my heart!
> Hysterica passio, down, thou climbing sorrow,
> Thy element's below....
> O me, my heart, my rising heart! but, down!

The third shock, the rejection by Regan, follows immediately. Lear prays for patience; he threatens revenges—the terrors of the earth—on the two daughters; his refusal to ease his heart by weeping is accompanied by the first rumblings of the storm which is a projecting on the macrocosm of the tempest in the microcosm; and he knows from the thunder that what he most feared will come to pass: 'O fool, I shall go mad!' Exposure to the storm completes what ingratitude began.

Lear's identification with the storm is both a means of presenting it on the stage and a sign that his passions have overthrown his reason. He contends 'with the fretful elements';

> tears his white hair,
> Which the impetuous blasts, with eyeless rage,
> Catch in their fury, and make nothing of;
> Strives in his little world of man to out-storm
> The to-and-fro-conflicting wind and rain.

But when Lear makes his next appearance, invoking the storm to destroy the seeds of matter, urging the gods to find out their hidden enemies, or addressing the poor naked wretches, he is not yet wholly mad, though he admits that his wits are beginning to turn. What finally pushes him over the borderline is the sudden appearance of Poor Tom who is both a living embodiment of naked poverty and one who is apparently what Lear had feared to become. Edgar, in acting madness, precipitates Lear's.

> What! have his daughters brought him to this pass?
> Could'st thou save nothing? Didst thou give 'em all?...
> Is it the fashion, that discarded fathers
> Should have thus little mercy on their flesh?
> Judicious punishment! 'twas this flesh begot
> Those pelican daughters.

The Fool comments:

> This cold night will turn us all to fools and madmen.

It is in fact the exposure and the physical exhaustion which prevents Lear's recovery from the shocks he has received. He is soon trying to identify himself with unaccommodated man by tearing off his clothes.

The madness of the elements, the professional 'madness' of the Fool, the feigned madness of Edgar, and the madness of the King himself together exemplify the break-up of society and the threat to the universe itself under the impact of ingratitude and treachery. When

Gloucester appears, confessing that he is almost mad and that grief for his son's treachery has crazed his wits, only Kent is left wholly sane.

Poor Tom compares himself with emblematic animals—hog, fox, wolf, dog and lion—and Lear contrasts the naked Bedlam, who does not borrow from worm, beast, sheep and cat, with the sophisticated people who do. Man without the refinements of civilization is 'a poor, bare, forked animal', as man without reason is no more than a beast. But Lear, who has lost his reason, is anxious to discuss philosophical questions with the man he takes for a learned Theban. His first question, 'What is the cause of thunder?', had been a stock one ever since the days of Pythagoras, who had taught, Ovid tells us,

> The first foundation of the world: the cause of every thing:
> What nature was: and what was God: whence snow and lyghtning spring:
> And whether *Jove* or else the wynds in breaking clowdes doo thunder.[19]

The storm suggests the question to Lear.

Just as the cuckolded madman in *The Honest Whore* is obsessed by his wife's unfaithfulness, and just as Ophelia is obsessed by her father's death and by the warnings given by her father and brother about preserving her virginity, so Lear returns again and again to the thing which had driven him mad—his daughters' ingratitude. He asks if Poor Tom's daughters have brought him to this pass; he exclaims:

> Now, all the plagues that in the pendulous air
> Hang fated o'er men's faults light on thy daughters!—

declares that nothing but his unkind daughters 'could have subdu'd nature / To such a lowness'; and inveighs against the flesh which 'begot / Those pelican daughters'.

Just before he was driven out into the storm Lear had declared that he would avenge himself on his daughters:

> I will have such revenges on you both,
> That all the world shall—I will do such things,—
> What they are, yet I know not; but they shall be
> The terrors of the earth.

In the refuge provided by Gloucester Lear begins to brood on his revenge. But the echo from Harsnett[20] in the lines—

> To have a thousand with red burning spits
> Come hissing in upon 'em—

suggests that Lear may be thinking of his daughters being punished by devils in hell. If he is indulging in the fantasy of punishing them in this world, he suddenly decides to bring them to trial first. Poor Tom in his blanket, and the Fool in his motley, suggest to his disordered mind two robed men of justice, and he imagines—this is his first actual illusion—that he sees Goneril and Regan. When we remember Lear's later attacks on the operations of justice because the judges are as guilty as the criminals they try, the justices in the mock trial of Goneril and Regan—a Bedlam beggar, a Fool, and a serving-man—are at least as likely to deal justly as a properly constituted bench, even though Lear accuses them of corruption in allowing the criminals to escape.

Shakespeare hits on two characteristics of certain kinds of mental derangement—the substitution of a symbolic offence for a real one ('she kick'd the poor King her father') and the obsession with a visual image. Lear thinks of the 'warped looks' of Regan, though in an earlier scene he had spoken of her 'tender-hefted nature' and of her eyes which, unlike Goneril's, 'do comfort and not burn'. It was the contrast between her beauty and her behaviour when she, like Goneril, put on a frowning countenance, that impressed Lear with her warped looks; and the same contrast makes Lear ask:

Is there any cause in nature that makes these hard hearts?

The question is an appropriate introduction to the next scene in which we see the tender-hearted Regan assisting at the blinding of Gloucester.

When the imaginary curtains are drawn on the sleeping Lear[21] we do not see him again for nearly 500 lines—about half-an-hour's playing time—but we are prepared for the development of his lunacy by the two short scenes in the middle of the fourth Act. In one of these Kent reveals that Lear refuses to see Cordelia:

A sovereign shame so elbows him: his own unkindness,
That stripp'd her from his benediction, turn'd her
To foreign casualties, gave her dear rights
To his dog-hearted daughters, these things sting
His mind so venomously, that burning shame
Detains him from Cordelia.

It is significant—though I do not remember that anyone has called attention to it—that after the admission at the end of Act I 'I did her wrong', Lear makes no further reference to Cordelia until he recovers his wits at the end of Act IV. The reason for this is partly, no doubt, that the ingratitude of Goneril and Regan drives everything else from his mind; but we may suspect, too, that Lear's sovereign shame prevents him from facing his own guilt. In the other scene (IV, iv) Cordelia describes her mad father,

singing aloud;
Crown'd with rank fumiter and furrow weeds,
With burdocks, hemlock, nettles, cuckoo-flowers,
Darnel, and all the idle weeds that grow
In our sustaining corn.

The significance of this picture is that Lear has reverted to his childhood. The Doctor, like the Court physicians attending both Henry VIII for his *mal d'esprit* and Elizabeth for her 'stupor', prescribes rest for the lunatic king:[22]

Our foster-nurse of nature is repose,
The which he lacks; that to provoke in him,
Are many simples operative, whose power
Will close the eye of anguish.

His colleague at Dunsinane holds out no such hopes for Lady Macbeth. The perilous stuff which weighs upon her heart cannot be cleansed from her bosom. The doctor cannot minister

30

to a diseased mind. 'Therein the patient must minister to' herself. This is because her mental illness is caused by her mortal sin. 'More needs she the divine than the physician.' Timothy Bright, who was both physician and divine, distinguished clearly between a sense of guilt caused by neurosis and that caused by sin:

Whatsoeuer molestation riseth directly as a proper obiect of the mind, that in that respect is not melancholicke, but hath a farther ground then fancie, and riseth from conscience, condemning the guiltie soule of those ingrauen lawes of nature, which no man is voide of, be he neuer so barbarous. This is it, that hath caused the prophane poets to haue fained Hecates Eumenides, and the infernall furies; which although they be but fained persons, yet the matter which is shewed vnder their maske, is serious, true, and of wofull experience.[23]

In the scene in which the mad Lear meets the blinded Gloucester there is a wonderful blend of 'matter and impertinency'. Even the impertinency has the kind of free association which is often found in the utterances of certain types of lunatics; and precisely because he is mad Lear is freed from the conventional attitudes of society. He is able, at moments, to see more clearly and piercingly than the sane, because the sane buy their peace of mind by adjusting themselves to the received ideas of society. Lear recognizes the way he has been shielded from reality by flattery. He also sees the hypocritical pretensions of society with regard to sex and with regard to its treatment of criminals. And, finally, he sees that human life is inescapably tragic:

> Thou must be patient; we came crying hither;
> Thou know'st the first time that we smell the air,
> We wawl and cry...
> When we are born, we cry that we are come
> To this great stage of fools.

When we next see Lear he is awakening from a drugged sleep. The Doctor has given him the repose he needs. The second part of the cure consists of music which, as later with Pericles, was a means of winding up the untuned and jarring senses. The third part of the cure is Cordelia's love. It is characteristic of her that she is eloquent so long as Lear is asleep, and that she falls back into her natural reticence when he awakens. The cure is completed when he kneels to the daughter he has wronged and begs her forgiveness.

It has often been observed by doctors of widely differing views that Shakespeare is clinically accurate in his presentation of the symptoms of madness. The difference between Lear's madness and Ophelia's illustrates his extraordinary insight into different kinds of mental illness; and, moreover, the feigned madness of Edgar (suitable to the scenes in which it appears) is quite different from the feigned madness of Hamlet, suitable both to the character and to the situation, though neither would be mistaken by a competent alienist for real insanity. One has only to compare Webster's madmen in *The Duchess of Malfi* and *The White Devil*, or the more extended treatment of madness by Fletcher in *The Two Noble Kinsmen* or by Otway in *Venice Preserved* with Shakespeare's to see how immeasurably superior he is to his rivals in this respect. The mad speeches of Fletcher and Otway are irremediably 'literary', and they hardly need the parody of Sheridan's Tilburina to show up their unreality.

Many of Shakespeare's contemporaries believed that madness was often, if not always, the result of possession; but he himself treated only mistaken or feigned madness in this way. Antipholus is thought to be possessed; Malvolio, though known to be sane, is treated by Feste as though he were possessed; and Edgar pretends that he has been possessed.[24] It is significant that for Edgar's feigned lunacy Shakespeare drew on *A Declaration of Egregious Popish Impostures* in which Harsnett analysed the confessions of bogus demoniacs. It has been suggested[25] that Shakespeare shared the sceptical views of Reginald Scott and Samuel Harsnett on demonology and witchcraft. At least it may be said that the mental illness of Lear has nothing supernatural about it.

NOTES

1. *Tempest*, v, i, 60.
2. Bucknill's views are accessible in the New Variorum edition.
3. Somerville professes to diagnose the mental illnesses of a number of Shakespeare's characters—Macbeth, for example, being paranoiac, Timon a megalomaniac, and Othello impotent.
4. Cf. K. Muir, 'Freudian Interpretations of Shakespeare' (*Proceedings of the Leeds Philosophical and Literary Society*, 1952). Sharpe, *op. cit.* p. 218, says that the storm 'is an imaginative suggestion of an actual storm representing the psychical one raging in the mind of the poet'. The significance of the whole play is implicit in the opening dialogue between Gloucester and Kent (pp. 222 ff.): 'Gloucester recalls certain events in his past life, the happy intercourse with his wife and later the birth of his second son'. 'The poet, through Lear, reveals emotional reactions to the mother of his childhood and, more hidden and complicated, those experienced towards his father.' She goes on to suggest that 'mother-Goneril's pregnancy is the cause of child Lear's "storm"' in the play; that Lear's knights represent faeces; that during one of his mother's pregnancies Shakespeare became incontinent, and that during the next he ran away from home and was found decked with the flowers of late summer. Apart from any scepticism we may have of this biographical fantasy, it should be pointed out that as Joan Shakespeare was christened on April 15, 1569, her mother's pregnancy would not have been visible in the late summer of 1568. There are many other dubious interpretations in Sharpe's essay. Lear's decision to stay with each daughter a month in turn is ascribed, not to Shakespeare's sources, but to fantasies concerning Mrs John Shakespeare's menstruation. 'Goneril with a white beard' tells 'of repressed knowledge of menstruation, bandage, and pubic hair'. Oddest of all is the comment on Lear's death-scene: 'The symbolic surrender to the father is complete in his last request to the father-figure, "Pray you, undo this button". Kent replies: "Oh let him pass..." Father's heart is melted, he does not hate him. In that button undone, and the symbolic "passing" is clear enough the psychical homosexual retreat from the Œdipus conflict.'
5. D. G. James, *The Life of Reason* (1949), p. 149.
6. Cf. G. M. Young, *Shakespeare and the Termers* (1948).
7. M. Maeterlinck, *Life and Flowers* (1907), p. 200.
8. G. Orwell, *Selected Essays* (1957), p. 116.
9. Cf. *Hamlet*, III, iii, 11–23; *All's Well*, II, iii, 124 ff.
10. Cf. Ophelia's mad songs.
11. *Lear*, II, iv, 131–4.
12. *Lear*, III, ii, 49 ff.
13. *Lear*, III, iv, 28.
14. L. Schücking, *Character Problems in Shakespeare Plays* (1922), pp. 186–9.
15. K. Muir, ed. *Lear*, p. lx.
16. Cf. E. Welsford, *The Fool* (1935), *passim*; W. Empson, *The Structure of Complex Words* (1951), pp. 125–57; R. H. Goldsmith, *Wise Fools in Shakespeare* (1935), *passim*.
17. *The Honest Whore*, Part I, v, ii.
18. Cited in New Variorum edition.
19. *Metamorphoses* (trans. Golding), xv, 74 ff.

20. Cf. K. Muir, *Review of English Studies* (1951), pp. 11–21.

21. It has been suggested to me that when Lear falls asleep after his exposure to the storm he is incubating a cold, and that in the mad scene in Act IV he may display toxic delirium in addition to his mania; but, one would imagine, too long a time is supposed to have elapsed between the two scenes.

22. All physicians, however, were not so humane, and neither Henry VIII nor Elizabeth I were mad. George III, when he was insane, was beaten.

23. *A Treatise of Melancholy* (1586), sig. N1^r.

24. Possibly Shakespeare intended us to think, or was willing to let us think, that Lady Macbeth was possessed.

25. Henry N. Paul, *The Royal Play of 'Macbeth'* (1950), p. 130.

LEAR'S QUESTIONS

BY

WINIFRED M. T. NOWOTTNY

The greatness of *King Lear* is of a kind that almost disables criticism: in it, Shakespeare has so reconciled opposites as to make it difficult to frame any valid statement about the nature of the play as a whole. The total impression is one of primitive simplicity, of solid rock unfretted by the artist's tool, but whenever, in studying it, the mind is visited by some small insight into its pattern (for of course it is patterned), further reflexion swiftly brings about a rush of critical excitement over the widening significances of what seemed at first a detail of the design, and this not once but many times; life is not long enough fully to explore *King Lear*. These repeated experiences of the play should inure the critic to the idea that whatever element of its design seems at any given moment most fascinating it is none the less merely one element among many, and the critic will do well to think of himself as the groping speleologist who traverses, astonished, one only of the many levels of that rock whose hidden intricacies are no more impressive than its simple mass. It is the purpose of this article to consider Lear's habit of asking questions, and though this (at the moment) seems to me of fundamental importance in the play, it must be stressed that commentary on them is made in mindfulness of the fact that the play is inexhaustibly patterned, and any act of critical consideration of its patterns must be at best limited and in the last resort less true to the play as a whole than a perception of the final unified simplicity of its effect—or, one should perhaps say, of the powerful illusion of simplicity which the play's patterns promote and subserve.

King Lear, as far as his outward fortunes are concerned, is a passive hero, but at the same time he is himself the active cause of what is tragic (as distinct from pathetic) in his experience, and is indeed more truly the maker of his own tragedy, by virtue of the questions he himself raises, than any other Shakespearian tragic hero. The play opens with the *locus classicus* of Lear's questioning: "Which of you shall we say doth love us most?" Goneril's comment that Lear has "put himself from rest" is applicable to this and to almost every subsequent question he asks. It is applicable too, to the essential condition of man, and what in Lear's questioning is wilful is also what (being autonomous) lifts him clear of the particular circumstances of plot and personality and makes him that Everyman that Macbeth with his Witches, Othello with his Iago, even Hamlet with his Ghost, cannot be. In the light of Lear's subsequent questions the first question is seen to be no mere device to get the play started, for his subsequent questions are in a sense as wilful as the first, going beyond the immediate provocation of the moment in which he formulates them. In Act I, sc. iv, when Goneril is insolent, Lear instantly flies at the questions:

> Doth any here know me? This is not Lear:
> Doth Lear walk thus? speak thus? Where are his eyes?
> Either his notion weakens, his discernings
> Are lethargied—Ha! waking? 'tis not so.
> Who is it that can tell me who I am?

The Fool interjects, "Lear's shadow", to which Lear ironically assents:

I would learn that; for, by the marks of sovereignty, knowledge, and reason, I should be false persuaded I had daughters.

Thus upon the goad of Goneril's insolence he has immediately involved himself in two questions which run through the play: whether or not he possesses sovereignty and whether or not he truly knows anything. When (in Act II, sc. iv) Regan and Goneril deny him his "additions", Lear takes in a serious sense the canting "What need one?" of Regan, and argues with real concern the problem of "true need":

> Allow not nature more than nature needs,
> Man's life's as cheap as beast's: thou art a lady;
> If only to go warm were gorgeous,
> Why, nature needs not what thou gorgeous wear'st,
> Which scarcely keeps thee warm—

and though in the course of the play he comes to condemn as sophistication what he here defends, this passage is the beginning of his involvement with the question of "unaccommodated man". In this same speech he goes on to question the gods themselves:

> If it be you that stir these daughters' hearts
> Against their father, fool me not so much
> To bear it tamely;

—this is a problem which comes to the fore in the speeches he hurls against the storm. When, conducted to the hovel, he encounters Poor Tom, he demands "Is man no more than this?" Such questions, however strong the personal feelings that underlie them, are more searching than the situation itself necessitates. Similarly, at the very last, over the body of Cordelia, Lear will ask,

> Why should a dog, a horse, a rat, have life,
> And thou no breath at all?

These are the questions of a Prometheus, even though they begin in a family quarrel, and Shakespeare meant it so: Lear himself uses the Promethean image,

> she hath tied
> Sharp-toothed unkindness, like a vulture, here.

Before the end of Act II, all the problems that dominate the dialogue of Lear's scenes in Acts III and IV have been posed, and posed by Lear himself: the nature of his own status and identity, the nature of knowing, the nature of need, the nature of the gods; and Lear has also raised, though not as a direct question, the problem of the inherent guilt of the flesh:

> thou art my flesh, my blood, my daughter;
> Or rather a disease that's in my flesh,
> Which I must needs call mine: thou art a boil,
> A plague-sore, an embossed carbuncle,
> In my corrupted blood.

It is the grand achievement of Act III to connect these problems so closely that each increases another's momentum. Lear's own experiences in the storm provide the emotional and logical connexions. The dialogue with the storm is, clearly, a battle with the gods. Pitting himself against the heavens, Lear challenges them to reveal their nature and his own: is he their slave? or is it they who are servile ministers? But this speech, the climax of Lear's resistance to the evil directed against himself by Goneril and Regan, is at the same time but the prelude to deeper issues between the gods and men: are they in their wrath the punishers of covert guilt? and what of the "poor naked wretches" who are involved in "seasons such as these"? Here, though Lear defiantly asserts his own innocence,

I am a man
More sinn'd against than sinning—

this assertion is of short duration, giving place at once to his recognition that he himself has taken too little thought of needy man, and destined to give place again to a deepening of his insight into that "disease that's in my flesh, which I must needs call mine". In this apparently inconclusive struggle with the gods, he does find answers to questions he himself has already raised: that of the nature of man's knowing, and that of his own status. He finds out (as we are told later) that he had been deceived about himself and he finds out also (as we are told immediately) that true knowledge is born of what is felt in the flesh:

Take physic, pomp;
Expose thy self to feel what wretches feel.

From this it is a short step to the notion that the man who must "answer with [his] uncovered body this extremity of the skies" is at the heart of truth; Poor Tom because he is most exposed must feel most and so know most, and so he becomes Lear's "philosopher", of whom Lear asks, "What is the cause of thunder?" Through the impact of the storm Shakespeare has effected one of the most difficult acts of communication necessary to the subsequent development of the play: he has brought home to us Lear's belief that all a man can know is what he knows through the flesh. Further, in Lear's defiance of the storm, his involvement with the problem of guilt has been brought to the fore. By a master-stroke, Shakespeare now establishes an intimate relation between Lear's several preoccupations, by using for them all the one symbol of the flesh: the flesh that suffers, knows, begets, is punished for its guilt. This is strikingly done when Lear first encounters Poor Tom. His first speech connects the idea of punishing the flesh with the idea of begetting:

Is it the fashion, that discarded fathers
Should have thus little mercy on their flesh?
Judicious punishment! 'twas this flesh begot
Those pelican daughters.

His next speech connects the idea of the exposed and suffering flesh with the idea of real truth:

Why, thou wert better in thy grave than to answer with thy uncovered body this extremity of the skies. Is man no more than this?...here's three on's are sophisticated! Thou art the thing itself....Off, off, you lendings! come, unbutton here.

Gloucester in the same scene furthers the power of the symbol with his words,

> Our flesh and blood is grown so vile, my lord,
> That it doth hate what gets it.

Henceforward the language takes on the function of binding more closely and exploring more deeply the connexions set up by Lear's experiences in the storm. It is the discovery of the metonymy, "the flesh", wherewith to advert to all the problems vital to the play which gives the language of the latter part of the tragedy its characteristic mark of simplicity charged with power, for within the metonymic structure made possible by the use of this common term, Shakespeare is able to sweep the strings of feeling whilst seeming to make no gesture at all.

The language of the play is further shaped for Shakespeare's purposes by a deliberate exploitation of the ambivalence of this term and of the aptness of the symbol for development through cognate terms such as "heart", "hand", "eyes", "brains", which also, in common usage, have both abstract and concrete significance. Much of the sombre power of the most memorable utterances in the mad scenes is due to the subtle interplay between the flesh as mere flesh and the qualities the flesh embodies, and to the interplay between the different members of that whole complex of ideas of which the flesh has been made the symbol. For instance, Lear's sudden demand,

> Then let them anatomize Regan; see what breeds about her heart. Is there any cause in nature that makes these hard hearts?

is macabre, not merely gruesome, because of the interplay between abstract and concrete, coupled with the interplay between the multiple references of the symbol: the flesh itself when dissected will reveal the truth, but an *intellectual* truth ("anatomize" meant not only to dissect but also to give a reasoned analysis or enumeration of qualities); this flesh is also the flesh in which evil things "breed" and the flesh subject to Nature's laws, the flesh in which the physical and spiritual are, according to Lear, so wholly united that the "heart" that breeds wickedness is also the "heart" that can be dissected and its hardness probed to seek the final cause. And the form of this sudden demand is such that we can simultaneously accept it as natural to Lear's way of thinking, and reject it as unnatural to our own. This is but one example of the way in which the language of the mad scenes achieves metaphysical subtlety without breaking the illusion of naturalistic presentation. In the mad scenes Lear again and again has sombre utterances whose power to strike directly at the heart is due to the peculiar dexterity with which they walk the precipice between the figurative and the true, as in Lear's,

> Give me an ounce of civet, good apothecary, to sweeten my imagination:

or in his,

> Let me have surgeons;
> I am cut to the brains.

This technique is, I am convinced, deliberate, and it does much to produce that sense of inexplicable power which we feel in attending a performance of the play. This is of course tricky ground for the critic; Shakespeare here is using means which outstrip our analytical terms. But the belief that the sense of shifting relations between true and false given by these utterances is of definable importance to the total effect of these scenes is strengthened by the evident fact that the mad scene with Gloucester (IV, vi) is a sustained exercise in the deployment of multiple uncertainties, so consistent in this aspect of its technique as to leave no doubt of what is being done.

In the mad scene with Gloucester the dialogue deliberately inhabits a no-man's-land between truth and falsehood; it is this ("matter and impertinency mixed") that makes it the pregnant "reason in madness" it is. Lear's first remark sets the tone:

No, they cannot touch me for coining; I am the king himself. Nature's above art in that respect.

This speech, whose immediate reference, no doubt, is to the imaginary press-money he is about to hand out, at once strikes the note of an uncertain relation between the true and the false, a note with many overtones: Lear is coining money, but is no coiner, since he is the King himself (and this phrase recalls his uncertainty about whether and in what sense he may be called king) and being by nature a king (if he is a king at all) his creations are true, unlike the feignings of art—but at the same time what he is now creating (the press-money) *is* a figment, with which he "pays" the other figments of his brain. (It has been well said that the play "disables the reflective reason of the reader"; dialogue such as this, which moves between the real and the unreal, is one of the means by which that effect is produced). Then Lear in his fantasy asks for the password. A voice from the real world offers one at random. "Pass". Unnervingly, it is the right password. And, as Lear accepts Edgar as part of his fantasy, his voice reaches the dark world of the blind and deluded Gloucester:

I know that voice.

Lear wheels upon him, not seeing him—"Goneril"—yet somehow seeing him—"with a white beard!"—and at once the white beard suggests white hairs as a figure of wisdom, and he recalls the deception of his daughters:

They flattered me like a dog; and told me I had white hairs in my beard ere the black ones were there.

With mad shrewdness he reflects that their "'Ay' and 'no' too, was no good divinity", and the word "divinity" takes his mind to that battle of his own with the gods in which he found out about the gods and himself and, like a dog, smelt out Regan and Goneril too. "They told me I was every thing; 'tis a lie, I am not ague-proof." This summing-up of his experiences and problems, which makes excellent sense to Lear and sense enough to us (who have been made to understand how Lear has put the tests of the senses in the place of ordinary reason) means nothing to Gloucester, but the voice that delivers it does:

The trick of that voice I do well remember:
Is't not the king?

When Lear replies, "Ay, every inch a king", we feel that claim to be true, though the Lear who makes it is mad and destitute, and childish too, for he proves his kingship by his power to terrify:

When I do stare, see how the subject quakes,

thus taking us back beyond the kingly Lear of the storm to the Lear of the opening scenes. But immediately upon this, as he turns to interrogate another phantom of his brain, it is as a king who pardons where he might have condemned:

> I pardon that man's life. What was thy cause?
> Adultery?
> Thou shalt not die: die for adultery! No.

Yet it is a wry and immoral compassion, a compassion for man which is possible only when man is seen as no different from the animals ("The wren goes to't, and the small gilded fly Does lecher in my sight") and his copulation useful ("To't, luxury, pell-mell! for I lack soldiers"). Suddenly the sense of man's difference from the animals (moral responsibility) returns, and with it a sense of sin and a revulsion from the animality of the sinful flesh, the compassion giving way to "There's hell, there's darkness, there's the sulphurous pit, Burning, scalding, stench, consumption." The grotesque picture of woman's sexuality (the extremest point of Lear's sense of the sinfulness of the flesh) is not only in itself a tale of false appearances, of monstrosity in nature and of a grotesque conjunction of gods and devils, but also it is in the end rejected as the vapour of an imagination itself in need of something to disguise its own stench. Hard upon this passage, both full of revulsion and provocative of revulsion in the hearer, come the words of Gloucester, charged with reverence and love:

> O, let me kiss that hand!

and, at this, Lear achieves the most sombre and powerful of those utterances in which the flesh and the spirit mingle in bewildering relations:

> Let me wipe it first; it smells of mortality.

It seems to me that, except for the last scene of all, there is no greater moment in the play than this. Here Lear is seen with that profound humanism which recognizes man as being at once wondrous and frail: supreme object of love and reverence, to whom one says, "O, let me kiss that hand!" and yet by his very condition, one who "smells of mortality"; in brief, the "ruined [master]piece of nature". This is a moment of complete truth, the more powerful because it comes as the climax of a dialogue fraught with ambiguities, with reason in madness, with lightning traversings and inversions of the familiar categories of the true and the false. This interchange between Lear and Gloucester is an epiphany of that idea of man by which the whole tragedy is informed. Immediately, the dialogue veers off into ambiguities more fantastic than before. For instance, when Gloucester asks, "Dost thou know me?" Lear's reply, "I remember thine eyes well enough" is as wildly untrue as it could be and yet true in the sense that Lear understands well enough the cruelty that brought about Gloucester's blindness, and he goes on to the paradoxically true statement, "A man may see how this world goes with no eyes", which in turn introduces Lear's own "great image of authority", that of the rational creature who in this world must run from the cur, and the passage on social injustice which so clearly analyses the perversions of justice and yet is, in the very absoluteness of its condemnation, so falsified a picture (just as the passage on sexuality was part penetration and part extravagance) that Edgar is moved to comment,

> O, matter and impertinency mix'd!
> Reason in madness!

As suddenly the twisted truth of this passage gives place to lucidity—"I know thee well enough; thy name is Gloucester" and to a simple observation of real life, "Thou know'st, the first time that we smell the air, We wawl and cry" which is swiftly followed by the metaphysical gloss, "we cry that we are come To this great stage of fools", and then the scene dissolves in mad cunning: "Nay, if you get it, you shall get it by running" and is linked to normality (which must now follow) by the comment of the gentleman who stands by,

> A sight most pitiful in the meanest wretch,
> Past speaking of in a king!

This comment makes explicit another of the qualities of this scene. It is that scene in which Shakespeare brings to a maximum effect of dissonance all the problems of the play. The problem of suffering is at its rawest in this scene, where mad Lear confronts blinded Gloucester in a visible spectacle of which nothing can be said, save "it is, And my heart breaks at it", a scene in whose fragmented dialogue, which every now and then sharpens to a sliver that stabs the heart and brain, the problems that have brought Lear to this pass are restated in their extremest form. In complete destitution, he claims himself "every inch a king"; he recalls that Titanic struggle with the gods which taught him he had been flattered like a dog; his sense of the guilt of the flesh takes him down into the pit, and his sense of the guilt of "authority" lifts him to a height of compassion proper only to a suffering god ("None does offend, none, I say, none; I'll able 'em: Take that of me, my friend, who have the power To seal the accuser's lips"). This scene of maximum dissonance leads to that resolution of dissonance which in the reunion with Cordelia brings the play to a penultimate close of pure, still pathos. In that reunion, Lear's passion is over, "the great rage...is killed in him", and the plot comes full circle when he is restored to comfort, love and majesty—accepted, humbly, as undeserved gifts, by one claiming no more for himself than

I am a very foolish fond old man....Pray you now, forget and forgive: I am old and foolish.

These simple harmonies could not be as effective without the whirling dissonances of the mad scene with Gloucester. The simplicity of Lear's words in this scene could not be so moving were it not instinct with the memory of his long struggle to know the truth. The shifting relations between the false and the true, and between the physical 'real' and the non-physical 'real' now come to rest in such simple physical certainties as "I feel this pin prick"—certainties the more moving because they are now, to Lear, the only way he knows of settling those searching questions whose racking complexity has been revealed in the course of the play. We have come a long way from "Doth Lear walk thus? talk thus? where are his eyes?" to "I will not swear these are my hands", from "But goes thy heart with this?" to "Be your tears wet?"; all the wildness of the long journey is felt, quiescent now, in these questions and the simple physical tests by reference to which Lear finds some sort of answer. Similarly the simplicity of attitude, as in his hesitant,

41

"As I am a man, I think this lady To be my child Cordelia" is powerful because of all Lear has left behind him; he is no longer the wrathful dragon, the outraged king, the impotent revenger, the defiant Titan, the stoic, or the madman, but simply, now, a man. The daring of this is terrible. Shakespeare has made Lear, who has yet to face the worst, exhaust in advance every known tragic attitude (except that of self-destruction, but Gloucester has attempted and rejected that), leaving them all behind him. It is as though Shakespeare sought to write a tragedy which sets itself to present the bitterest experience of all without help of the trappings of tragic style or attitude. It is as man, not as tragic hero, that Lear is to meet the death of Cordelia—as man who has already of his own volition asked all the deepest metaphysical questions about man's condition, suffered all he could suffer because of them, and now, when "nature in [him] stands on the very verge Of her confine", confronts the one question he has so far escaped:

> Why should a dog, a horse, a rat, have life,
> And thou no breath at all?

And here the style, now in "a condition of complete simplicity, costing no less than everything" performs the final miracle of hardening from humble pathos to tragic rock by an intensification of its own simplicity: those same elements of which simple pathos was compounded, are compounded anew. Lear, so recently content to know so little, is now certain of the simplest, sharpest distinction of all: "I know when one is dead, and when one lives." A simple physical test, again, will settle the only question that matters: "Lend me a looking-glass; If that her breath will mist or stain the stone, Why then she lives." And if she lives, life even as he has known it makes sense:

> if it be so,
> It is a chance which does redeem all sorrows
> That ever I have felt.

And at the last, she seems to him to live.

The whole play is a dramatic answer to the one question in which all Lear's questions are subsumed: the question, What is Man? Man is that creature whose inherent nature is such as to raise the questions Lear asks; he is at once no more and no less than this, the creature at once vulnerable and tenacious, who must, but can, "answer with [his] uncovered body this extremity of the skies", the "ruined piece of nature" whose hand, smelling of mortality, is august, the creature whose mere life is so perfectly a value in itself that it redeems even those sorrows Lear has felt. This conception, explicit at the tragic peaks of the play, tacitly governs its whole structure. The sequence of Lear's deprivations is a sequence of revelations of his tenacity. It is to this end—revelation through suffering (rather than redemption through suffering)—that the whole play moves.

13. Act v scene iii: 'Come, let's away to Prison. / We two alone will sing like birds i' th' cage' (from *King Lear: The Space of Tragedy*, the diary of Grigori Kozintsev).

14. Act v scene iii: 'Cordelia, Cordelia! Stay a little. Ha! / What is't thou say'st?' Yuri Yarvet as Lear and Valentina Shendrikova as Cordelia (from *King Lear: The Space of Tragedy*, the diary of Grigori Kozintsev).

11. Act IV scene vi: ''Tis the times' plague when madmen lead the blind'. Grigori Kozintsev's film of *King Lear*, 1970, with Yuri Yarvet as Lear, K. Cebric as Gloucester and Lionard Merzin as Edgar (from *King Lear: The Space of Tragedy*, the diary of Grigori Kozintsev).

12. Act IV scene vii: 'Be your tears wet?' Louise Jameson as Cordelia and Tony Church as Lear in Buzz Goodbody's production at The Other Place, 1974.

8. Act II scene iv. Paul Scofield as Lear with Goneril, 1962.

9. Act III scene ii: the storm. Charles Laughton as Lear, Ian Holm as the Fool, Shakespeare Memorial Theatre 1959.

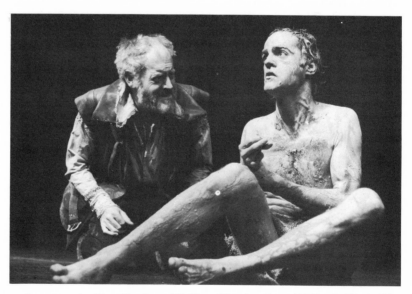

10. Act III scene iv: 'Poor Tom's a-cold': Tony Church as Lear and Mike Gwilym as Edgar in Buzz Goodbody's production at The Other Place, 1974.

Painting on the West Face of the Wall which divides the Nave from the Chancel of the Chapel of the Trinity at STRATFORD upon AVON in WARWICKSHIRE

3. Wall painting of the Last Judgement (Guild Chapel, Stratford-upon-Avon).

(a) Fuseli's 'Lear and Cordelia', Rivington's edition, 1805

(b) James Barry, from a painting for the Boydell Gallery, engraved by Legat

(c) Mulready drawing for Lamb's *Tales from Shakespeare*

(d) From Ford Madox Brown's 'Lear and Cordelia'

(e) Bernard Partridge: Irving as Lear

(f) Sir John Gielgud, *King Lear*, Stratford, 1956

(g) Robert Colquhoun, *King Lear*, Stratford, 1953

2. Costumes for productions of *King Lear*.

(*a*) From Rowe's frontispiece, 1709

(*b*) From Rowe's frontispiece, 1714

(*c*) From Hayman's frontispiece for Hanmer's Shakespeare, 1744

(*d*) From McArdell's mezzotint after Benjamin Wilson: 'Garrick as Lear'

(*e*) From van Bleeck: Mrs Cibber in Nahum Tate's adaptation of *King Lear*

(*f*) From John Runciman's 'Lear in the Storm', 1767

(*g*) Alexander Runciman, 'Lear on the Heath'

1. Costumes for productions of *King Lear*.

'AND THAT'S TRUE TOO': 'KING LEAR' AND THE TENSION OF UNCERTAINTY

DEREK PEAT

'By the end of *King Lear*, we should see that Cordelia possesses everything that is genuinely worth having.' This might be a quotation from *Shakespearean Tragedy*, but it comes from a recent book by John Reibetanz.[1] The approach is new, but the conclusions are familiar: 'through his sufferings Lear has won an enlightened soul'; 'we protest so strongly against Cordelia's death because we are not of her world'; 'Material goods are fetters and the body a husk to be discarded so that the fruit can be reached.'[2] Reibetanz acknowledges the obvious debt to Bradley, but he is no ordinary disciple. He admits his master's weaknesses, and emphasises them by considering precisely those areas Bradley ignored: the nature of the public and private theatres; Shakespeare's use and adaptation of contemporary stage tradition and the expectations of an audience moulded by regular playgoing. In the light of this, it is ironic that he reaches similar conclusions to the man who argued the play was 'too huge for the stage'.[3] Much less ironic is the fact that while I find most of Reibetanz's commentary thoroughly convincing, it leads me to an exactly opposite conclusion.

This is not so surprising; a survey of the criticism reveals it is in the nature of *King Lear* to stimulate contrary responses. There is a marked division between critics for whom the play makes an 'affirmation' and those who believe it does not.[4] Reibetanz, who argues that the play 'definitely points us to'[5] Christian doctrine, obviously belongs with the former

group, and I had better admit now that my own sympathies lie with the other side. This division of critical opinion is in itself, I believe, a direct result of the fact that *King Lear* forces every spectator to choose between the contrary possibilities it holds in unresolved opposition. Norman Rabkin's idea of the working of any Shakespearian play is an exact description of this particular one: 'the dramatic structure sets

[1] John Reibetanz, *The Lear World: A Study of King Lear in its Dramatic Context* (Toronto, 1977), p. 121.

[2] *Ibid.*, pp. 108, 122, 121.

[3] A. C. Bradley, *Shakespearean Tragedy* (1904; repr. 1969), p. 202.

[4] L. C. Knights uses the word 'affirmation' in the essay in *Some Shakespearean Themes* (London, 1959), but following Bradley's idea of '*The Redemption of King Lear*' (p. 235), many critics have argued that the ending is positive because Lear is redeemed through suffering. Several of these interpretations view *King Lear* as a 'Christian' play: Oscar James Campbell, 'The Salvation of Lear', *English Literary History*, 15 (1948); John F. Danby, *Shakespeare's Doctrine of Nature* (1949); Terence Hawkes, *Shakespeare and the Reason* (1964); R. B. Heilman, *This Great Stage* (Baton Rouge, 1948) and G. Wilson Knight, *The Wheel of Fire* (1959).

On the other side are those who find no evidence of redemption and who stress the horrors of the final scene. Among the most notable are: W. R. Elton, *King Lear and the Gods* (San Marino, Calif., 1966); Barbara Everett, 'The New *King Lear*', *Critical Quarterly*, 2 (1960); Helen Gardner, *King Lear* (John Coffin Memorial Lecture, 1967); S. L. Goldberg, *An Essay on King Lear* (Cambridge, 1974); John Holloway, *The Story of The Night* (1961) and Marvin Rosenberg, *The Masks of King Lear* (Berkeley, Los Angeles and London, 1972).

[5] Reibetanz, *The Lear World*, p. 120.

43

up opposed elements as equally valid...and equally destructive, so that the choice that the play forces the reader to make becomes impossible'.[1] Others have noticed this tension of irresolution. For J. D. Rosenberg 'each assertion in the play confronts a counter-assertion and all interpretations contain the seed of their refutation',[2] and S. L. Goldberg puts it this way: 'The outline of one thing is the boundary of its counterpart.'[3] The penultimate scene reveals the working of the play in microcosm:

Edgar.
  Here, father, take the shadow of this tree
  For your good host; pray that the right may thrive.
  If ever I return to you again,
  I'll bring you comfort.
Gloucester.   Grace go with you, sir! [*Exit Edgar.*
  Alarum; afterwards a retreat. Re-enter Edgar.
Edgar.
  Away, old man! give me thy hand: away!
  King Lear hath lost, he and his daughter ta'en.
  Give me thy hand; come on.
Gloucester.
  No further, sir; a man may rot even here.
Edgar.
  What! in ill thoughts again? Men must endure
  Their going hence, even as their coming hither:
  Ripeness is all.   Come on.
Gloucester.   And that's true too.   [*Exeunt.*
                              (v, ii, 1–11)[4]

Edgar asks for prayer and Gloucester gives his blessing, but 'the right' do not thrive. Before the battle Edgar is certain of victory and makes a strong assertion, only to have the action contradict him. The audience's expectation of a happy ending, fueled by the reconciliation between the King and his daughter (and for Shakespeare's contemporaries supported by memories of Leir and Cordella's victory in the old play) is abruptly reversed. Since the faked 'miracle' at Dover cliff, many of Gloucester's lines have indicated patient acceptance of his lot, yet here he reverts to despair. Most important of all, in a play which questions everything and depends upon right choice, is the way the scene ends. Contrary positions are given equal validity and Gloucester's reply to Edgar's famous remark might stand as the epigraph for the play: 'And that's true too.'

The point at which this process of juxtaposition comes to its climax is, appropriately enough, the moment when Lear dies:

  Why should a dog, a horse, a rat, have life,
  And thou no breath at all? Thou'lt come no more,
  Never, never, never, never, never!
  Pray you, undo this button: thank you, Sir.
  Do you see this? Look on her, look, her lips,
  Look there, look there!   (v, iii, 306–11)

There are two distinct possibilities: either Lear dies believing Cordelia lives, or his heart breaks as he realises the shattering reality of her death. The possibilities open up a variety of interpretations. A Lear who believes Cordelia is alive may be transcending earthly limitations, suffering under the final self-deception of a man who still 'but slenderly' knows himself, or taking refuge from reality in madness. In contrast, an awareness of Cordelia's death may be the culmination of a process of deepening knowledge of the self and the world. There is, of course, a third possibility, that Lear dies uncertain whether his daughter is alive or dead.

The text supports all these possibilities. The five times repeated 'never' seems conclusive enough, but since his entrance with Cordelia in his arms, the king has had other speeches which move from statement through qualification to counter-statement:

  She's dead as earth. Lend me a looking-glass;
  If that her breath will mist or stain the stone,
  Why, then she lives...
  This feather stirs; she lives!   (v, iii, 261–3, 265)

[1] Norman Rabkin, *Shakespeare and the Common Understanding* (New York and London, 1967), p. 12.
[2] John D. Rosenberg, 'King Lear and his Comforters', *Essays in Criticism*, 16 (1966), 144.
[3] S. L. Goldberg, *An Essay on King Lear* (Cambridge, 1974), p. 163.
[4] References are to the New Arden edition, ed. Kenneth Muir (1952; repr. 1967).

His final lines can be read as a similar move from one certainty to another, or as another example of his uncertainty.

The contradictory nature of the text is mirrored in the original editions. My quotation is the Folio version, but the Quarto omits the last two lines and contains the printer's formula for a death cry, 'O,o,o,o.' which suggests the king howling in anguish at his daughter's death. In the absence of evidence showing which ending Shakespeare favoured (if, indeed, both are his) all we can say is that while the Quarto supports one reading, the Folio allows others.

J. K. Walton makes his decision about the final lines after an examination of Lear's character and the development of the play. He concludes: 'If we take it that Lear finally believes that Cordelia is alive, we alter the direction of the whole movement which has been taking place throughout the play, a movement by which he attains to an even greater consciousness.'[1] Quite so, but in this play of reversals is there any reason to suppose Shakespeare did not 'alter the direction' himself? In the penultimate scene Gloucester reverses a parallel 'movement' in the subplot, and in this play subplot often mirrors main plot. In fact, as J. Stampfer points out, Gloucester's death 'twixt two extremes of passion' can parallel Lear dying torn between his realisation of death and hope of life.[2] The play provides evidence to support conflicting interpretations of Lear's last lines and it is not putting the cart before the horse to suggest that the decision we make about those lines finally determines the 'direction of the whole movement' of the play.

In performance what the audience see during Lear's death speech plays a major part in determining this decision. The actor responds to the change of tone after the final sonorous 'never' and there is a moment's pause as the button is undone. If this button is at Cordelia's throat, it may open to reveal the lacerations of the noose. Perhaps her mouth, to which Lear draws attention, falls open and utters 'nothing', not as a word but as an enduring silence. The relative stage positions, with the three daughters again surrounding their father, may complete the connection with the opening scene.[3] Or the button may be at Lear's throat which makes his transition to Cordelia's body logical as the king, gasping for air, remembers his hanged daughter. Lear may remember something else. After his experience of 'unaccommodated man', the 'this' to which he draws attention may be his own flesh. If a supernumerary undoes the button, the king may appear subdued and clear-eyed, but if he addresses Kent as 'Sir', the audience may see a man losing his grip on reality. At this point blocking is of crucial importance. If Lear stands close to Cordelia, or kneels clasping her, his death is at the focus of the audience's attention, but the effect is quite different if he moves away to have the button undone. Then, his insistent commands turn the attention of all onstage, and of the audience, towards the body and away from himself. The shock of his death is far greater if, as he falls, heads are turned away. The final lines may not refer to Cordelia at all. In Peter Brook's production,[4] Paul Scofield sat staring out blankly into the auditorium on his last 'look there'. In death his eyes remained open.

In his study of the play,[5] Marvin Rosenberg describes several other ways in which the death has been portrayed, but even my simplified list

[1] J. K. Walton, 'Lear's Last Speech', *Shakespeare Survey 13* (Cambridge 1960), p. 14.

[2] J. Stampfer, 'The Catharsis of *King Lear*', *Shakespeare Survey 13* (Cambridge, 1960), p. 4.

[3] Harley Granville-Barker noted this connection in his Preface. See *Prefaces to Shakespeare* (1947; repr. Princeton, 1965), pp. 17–18.

[4] Stratford-upon-Avon, 1962. The treatment of this moment in Brook's film of *King Lear* was quite different.

[5] Rosenberg, *The Masks of King Lear*, pp. 318–21.

makes it clear that, working from the contrary possibilities of one key speech (and I've said nothing about *how* the lines are delivered) we can create several different plays. One of them was suggested by Bradley who believed an actor should 'express, in Lear's last accents and gestures and look, an unbearable *joy*' because he thought Cordelia alive: 'To us, perhaps, the knowledge that he is deceived may bring a culmination of pain: but, if it brings *only* that, I believe we are false to Shakespeare.'[1] Some years ago, Maynard Mack argued along similar lines: 'Lear's joy in thinking that his daughter lives (if this is what his words imply) is illusory, but it is one we need not begrudge him...in a similar instance among our acquaintances, we would regard the illusion as a godsend, or even, if we were believers, as God-sent.'[2] Bradley was a believer: 'Let us renounce the world, hate it, and lose it gladly. The only real thing in it is the soul, with its courage, patience and devotion. And nothing outward can touch that.'[3] This is magnificent, but it is essentially the response of a reader who has divorced the play's meaning from its immediate effect in the theatre. Despite his insistence on the dramatic context, Reibetanz does something similar when he states: 'we should see Cordelia possesses everything that is genuinely worth having'. Perhaps we 'should', but I can't believe many spectators do.

Bradley, Mack and Reibetanz all share an assumption vital for their readings of the play: that the audience view Lear's final moments from a position of relative detachment and are, therefore, fully aware of the true facts of the situation. But what if the audience share the king's uncertainty? If they too look at Cordelia expecting some sign of life and find none as Lear falls, they are unlikely to view his death as a 'godsend' or to acknowledge that Cordelia has 'everything'. The audience may feel *they* have nothing.

King Lear opens with a discussion about an impossible choice:

Kent. I thought the King had more affected the Duke of Albany than Cornwall.
Gloucester. It did always seem so to us; but now, in the division of the kingdom, it appears not which of the Dukes he values most; for equalities are so weigh'd that curiosity in neither can make choice of either's moiety.
(i, i, 1–7)

Two possibilities are equalised and the play opens on a note of uncertainty. As the action develops, questions of 'choice' and 'value' become of paramount importance and the uncertainty intensifies, as Shakespeare leads the audience ever deeper into a world where they too must choose. Marvin Rosenberg suggests 'The *Lear* world is a world of uncertainties',[4] but these uncertainties do not just exist within the play, they are generated within the audience. Shakespeare continually confounds their expectations and, at times, makes it almost impossible for them to determine what is happening onstage and why. The uncertainty that results reaches its climax in the final moments of the play. A full substantiation of these claims would require a great deal more space than this essay permits, so I will limit myself to a detailed analysis of part of act iv scene vi, Gloucester's fall from Dover cliff, and then return to the moment of Lear's death to offer an alternative to Reibetanz's 'affirmative' reading.[5]

[1] Bradley, *Shakespearean Tragedy*, p. 241.
[2] Maynard Mack, *King Lear in Our Time* (1966), p. 116.
[3] Bradley, *Shakespearean Tragedy*, p. 273.
[4] Rosenberg, *The Masks of King Lear*, p. 6.
[5] In what follows I attempt to see the play from the viewpoint of a spectator who knows nothing of *King Lear* in order to recover something of its initial effect. I am indebted to Marvin Rosenberg's concept of the 'naive spectator' which he used in his work on the play, but did not describe in full until his recent study of *Macbeth* (*The Masks of Macbeth*, Berkeley, 1978). While I owe much to his insights and method, I think his approach holds some dangers – he stages the play before audiences who have never seen it before,

The scene on Dover cliff caused Bradley to make an uncharacteristic point: 'contrary to expectation, it is not, if properly acted, in the least absurd on the stage'. He added: 'The imagination and the feelings have been worked upon with such effect...that we are unconscious of the grotesqueness of the incident for common sense.'[1] Modern criticism has moved the other way. After G. Wilson Knight's formative essay 'King Lear and the Comedy of the Grotesque',[2] the elements Bradley denied, the grotesque and the absurd, are those that are emphasised. Jan Kott has even read the scene in terms of contemporary absurd drama.[3]

How does the scene affect an audience? Do the spectators believe Gloucester is at the edge of a cliff? Alan C. Dessen gives a representative answer: 'the fictional nature of the plummet from the cliff would be obvious to the audience'.[4] Admittedly, in performance, the fact that there is no cliff is usually made obvious, but it strikes me that the working of the scene depends on our remaining confused about the existence of cliff and sea.[5] Obviously, what the spectators see onstage is of primary importance. John Cranford Adams required some form of visual illusion and suggested that at the Globe Gloucester climbed a ramp – the property 'mossbank' – and several other critics have felt the need for a symbolic indication of height.[6] Jan Kott is content with a flat stage: 'Edgar...lifts his feet high pretending to walk uphill. Gloster too lifts his feet as if expecting the ground to rise, but underneath his foot there is only air.'[7] Neither the property nor the pantomime is necessary and without them the scene achieves a powerful ambivalence.

As it opens Gloucester poses the question about their true location:

Gloucester.
When shall I come to th' top of that same hill?
Edgar.
You do climb up it now; look how we labour.

Gloucester.
Methinks the ground is even.
Edgar.   Horrible steep:
Hark! do you hear the sea?
Gloucester.   No, truly.
Edgar.
Why, then your other senses grow imperfect
By your eyes' anguish.   (IV, vi, 1–6)

Of course, on the platform stage the 'ground' is 'even' and we could point to the exaggeration on 'horrible' as a clue that what Edgar states is untrue, but there is an obvious disagreement and, unless he is given some clear visual indication by the actor playing Edgar, a spectator unfamiliar with the play could not be

his 'naive spectators', and then questions them about their reactions. He probably takes into account changes in language, culture, theatrical traditions and architecture that all modify the play's effect, but even his word 'naive' is revealing. I assume the original spectators were far from this. I assume they recognised references to other plays and to contemporary events and that their expectations of the probable development of a play they were attending were moulded as much by their experience of similar plays, as by the play in hand. Shakespeare, like any dramatist working in a living tradition, could depend on this. He traded on their sophistication rather than their naivete.

[1] Bradley, *Shakespearean Tragedy*, p. 203.
[2] G. Wilson Knight, *The Wheel of Fire* (1930).
[3] Jan Kott, *Shakespeare Our Contemporary* (1967).
[4] Alan C. Dessen, 'Two Falls and a Trap', *English Literary Renaissance*, 5 (1975), pp. 291–307, p. 303.
[5] See my 'G. Wilson Knight and "Gloucester's Leap"', *Essays in Criticism*, 23 (1973), pp. 198–200.
[6] John Cranford Adams, 'The Original Staging of *King Lear*', *Folger Shakespeare Library Joseph Quincey Adams Memorial Studies* (1948), p. 330. Alvin B. Kernan favours a 'low step', 'Formalism and Realism in Elizabethan Drama: the Miracles of *King Lear*', *Renaissance Drama*, 9 (1966), p. 60. Waldo F. McNeir prefers a fall from 'a booth stage', 'The Staging of the Dover Cliff Scene in *King Lear*', *Studies in English Renaissance Drama*, ed. McNeir (Baton Rouge, 1962), p. 97. Harry Levin opts for 'a single step or a low platform', 'The Heights and the Depths: a scene from *King Lear*', *More Talking of Shakespeare*, ed. John Garrett (New York, 1959), p. 98. Dessen has a useful discussion of all these views and he favours a flat stage.
[7] Kott, *Shakespeare Our Contemporary*, pp. 112–13.

sure. Then follows Edgar's long and vividly descriptive speech on the view from the cliff. On the bare Jacobean stage with its scant properties, Shakespeare often sketches the scenery for the audience in a similar way. Normally, there is a consensus of opinion: what one character sees the others see and the audience therefore know the scene is as described. Here, Shakespeare uses the convention to secure a further effect, because Edgar describes the scene for a blind man who cannot corroborate the information. The audience are thus forced to make their own decision. Even Edgar's explanatory comment, 'Why I do trifle thus with his despair/Is done to cure it', gives no indication that the scene he described is not real, although it does raise other riddling questions. Just what is he up to? Does he intend to prevent Gloucester from jumping, or does he hope his father will change his mind if given enough time? An unfamiliar spectator may well think Edgar means to cast off his disguise at the last moment.[1] The text offers just such a possibility on Gloucester's final lines before the fall: 'If Edgar live, O, bless him!/Now, fellow, fare thee well.' Edgar remains disguised and Gloucester falls.

For Shakespeare's contemporaries the shock must have been immense, because nothing had prepared them to expect this. In the source story in Sidney's *Arcadia*, the Paphlagonian king's son refuses a request to lead his father to the edge of a cliff, and this cures the king's despair for a time. Shakespeare reverses the source and this is not the only reversal here. Would the spectators recognise in Edgar and Gloucester an emblem of the Devil tempting Christ to leap down from the pinnacle of the Temple? If they did not think of this initially, they surely would later when Edgar suggests 'It was some fiend' that led Gloucester to the edge. In the Bible, the Devil promises that Christ will be unharmed if he jumps, but the whole point of the story is that Christ refuses the temptation. This is by no means the only reversal of a religious image in the play. The greatest of them all is the reversed Pieta after Lear enters with Cordelia in his arms (the daughter has earlier associated herself with 'the Son' in an echo of Luke, ii, 49: 'O dear father,/ It is thy business that I go about'). For the contemporary audience, the sight of a man damning his soul with a blessing on his lips must have had an impact it is hard for us to imagine.

At this point, then, perhaps the spectators are not struck by the 'grotesque comedy', but terrified by the possibility that Gloucester has actually fallen from a cliff. It is only now, *after the event*, that Edgar reveals it is all an illusion:

And yet I know not how conceit may rob
The treasury of life when life itself
Yields to the theft; had he been where he thought
By this had thought been past.   (IV, vi, 42–5)

As Edgar has trifled with Gloucester, so Shakespeare has trifled with his audience. What he presents is so ambiguous that, to an extent, they are placed in Gloucester's situation: they too must trust the eyes and word of another, because they can't see for themselves.

Edgar's lines resolve the uncertainty about the cliff, but how are they spoken? Does he look on impassively as his father attempts suicide (did he expect him to jump?), or even though there is no real danger is he aware that he gambles with a human life? His next lines suggest the latter, as Shakespeare makes everything uncertain once more. Perhaps a man may die if he merely believes he has fallen from a cliff: 'Alive or dead?/Ho, you sir! friend! Hear you, sir! speak!' (ll. 45–6). For a moment the audience share the mounting anxiety evident in the broken rhythm, but Gloucester is not dead: 'Thus might he pass indeed; yet he revives.'

[1] Rosenberg, *The Masks of King Lear*, p. 264.

The scene is obviously a great theatrical *tour de force*, perfectly geared to the stage for which Shakespeare wrote: an open stage surrounded by the audience, on which illusion was created by the actors not by scenery. The proscenium stage is so much a part of the theatre of visual illusion that I suspect the scene can never attain its full power upon it. This may be why John D. Rosenberg finds it 'a remarkable piece of virtuoso stagecraft that does not quite come off'.[1] I don't agree, but I think his uncertainty is a direct response to Shakespeare's creation, because this scene exhibits precisely that tension created by contrary possibilities of which I spoke earlier. It strains the resources of the theatrical illusion to breaking point and there are few moments when our 'willing suspension of disbelief' is challenged so directly. How can an audience believe a flat stage is a hill? How can they believe Edgar when they know he is already involved in a deception? They are reminded of this at the scene's beginning and Gloucester's suspicion might well suggest that all Edgar states is untrue:

Edgar.
...your other senses grow imperfect
By your eyes' anguish.
Gloucester.   So may it be, indeed.
Methinks thy voice is alter'd, and thou speak'st
In better phrase and matter than thou didst.
Edgar.
You're much deceiv'd; in nothing am I chang'd
But in my garments.
Gloucester.   Methinks you're better spoken.
(IV, vi, 5–10)

Then, as Gloucester seems on the point of some discovery, Edgar describes the view from the cliff. If his father hears the change in Edgar's voice, but doesn't hear the sea, then the sea doesn't exist. Or does it? The audience's attitude shares something of the duality of Gloucester's 'And that's true too': they half believe the cliff is real while half suspecting it is all an illusion. John Cranford Adams comes

close to my perception of their double-vision: 'listening with Gloucester's ears the audience will share his illusion...Looking with Edgar's eyes, however, they will know that no precipice exists.' This expresses something of the tension I find in the scene, but for Adams the balance has already settled: 'Never for a moment is the audience expected to believe that Edgar has brought Gloucester to the edge of the Cliffs.'[2] My point is that the scene precludes such certainty. Until after the fall, Shakespeare does not allow the audience to make up their minds.

The *tour de force* continues as Edgar convinces his father that everything the audience suspected was real, is real indeed. There is much more that could be said of this amazing piece of theatre, but I want especially to note the way Shakespeare leaves the audience in uncertainty for so long and then allows them to witness a character who seemed dead return to life.

The final appearance of Lear with his daughter in his arms is an enormously powerful image. It has become a theatrical tradition that the severed noose hangs from Cordelia's neck, but the tradition begs the question: do the audience believe she is dead? The direction in both Quarto and Folio, 'Enter Lear with Cordelia in his arms', leaves this question open, but the reader of a modern edition may find the issue prejudiced by editors who follow Rowe and insert the word 'dead' after 'Cordelia'. In the theatre there are no such signposts.

The preparations for Lear's last entrance have been carefully made. Edgar's return from the battle (v, ii) is the first of a series of shock entrances that culminate in the king's final appearance. From this point, Shakespeare creates tension between an awareness of impending catastrophe and the possibility of a 'happy' resolution. As John Reibetanz suggests, the audience are 'suspended between hope and

[1] Rosenberg, 'King Lear and his Comforters', p. 142.
[2] Adams, 'The Original Staging of *King Lear*', p. 330.

despair' because 'Shakespeare invites a kind of double perspective: we follow the action as it progresses towards both its actual and its possible conclusions.' This seems to me exactly right, but Reibetanz adds: 'and we wait with some anxiety for the final stroke that will determine the shape of the whole'.[1] No audience in the theatre remains so detached: during this scene of mounting suspense, their emotion is intense. At the end, detachment is precisely what they are denied.

As the last scene opens, Shakespeare establishes the dual response the action will continue to evoke. Lear's 'birds i' th' cage' speech inspires hope, but while they respond to the beauty of the words, the audience remain aware of another listener, Edmund. His presence casts doubt on Lear's vision – he has already announced that the king 'Shall never see' Albany's pardon (v, i, 65–8) – and he interrupts with the voice of stark reality: 'Take them away' (v, iii, 19). Tension mounts throughout the scene as the pendulum swings between hope and despair. Immediately after Edmund despatches the murderer, hopes revive when Albany demands the captives, only to be damned again by Edmund's politic answer:

> . . . they are ready
> To-morrow, or at further space, t'appear
> Where you shall hold your session. At this time
> We sweat and bleed . . .   (v, iii, 53–6)

and the Captain has instructions to act 'instantly'. Albany maintains the possibility that 'right may thrive' by arresting Edmund and offering to fight himself, if the challenger fails to appear. As he predicted, the forces of evil begin to prey on one another as Regan succumbs to Goneril's poison, but what has happened to Lear and Cordelia? The question remains unanswered as Shakespeare creates other sources of suspense and uncertainty. The challenger must 'appear *by* the third sound of the trumpet'.[2] The trumpet sounds, but no one appears. As Albany is about to step forward, a trumpet sounds within and a man in armour enters. A spectator unfamiliar with the play may guess this is Edgar, but he cannot be sure, even when he hears this master-of-many-voices speak. After Lear's unexpected defeat, the audience must wonder whether the challenger can win. In his film version, Peter Brook imaged the uncertainty by dressing the brothers in identical armour, so it was impossible to distinguish which was which. Albany's cry 'Save him! save him!' (l. 151) is certainly given point if he cannot determine who is down.

Edgar's victory boosts the audience's hopes, but the unrepentant Edmund tips the balance the other way:

> What you have charg'd me with, that have I done,
> And more, much more; the time will bring it out:
> 'Tis past, and so am I.   (v, iii, 162–4)

Perhaps it is already too late. The possibility of salvation recedes during Edgar's long explanatory speech, and the audience are torn 'twixt two extremes of passion' as they hear Edmund's tantalising response to the news of Gloucester's death:

> This speech of yours has mov'd me,
> And shall perchance do good; but speak you on;
> You look as you had something more to say.
>   (v, iii, 199–201)

Edgar seems to be about to announce the king's fate:

> This would have seem'd a period
> To such as love not sorrow; but another,
> To amplify too much, would make much more,
> And top extremity.
> Whilst I was big in clamour came there in a man
>   (v, iii, 204–8)

but he brought no news of Lear. It was Kent who, like Gloucester, breaks under the power of emotion: 'His grief grew puissant, and the strings of life/Began to crack' (ll. 216–17).

[1] Reibetanz, *The Lear World*, p. 115.
[2] The Folio reading. In the Quarto, no trumpet answers within and Edgar enters '*at* the third sound'. The business recorded in Folio seems calculated to increase suspense.

Edgar 'left him tranc'd' and the audience suspect he has joined the growing ranks of death. Suddenly a man rushes on with a bloody knife and Shakespeare engineers the moment so the audience think Cordelia is dead, but it is Goneril's death he announces, so hope remains. Then comes an even more startling entrance: Kent appears. As the climax approaches, hope and despair are held in almost simultaneous opposition and Kent's entrance is a case in point. It promotes hope because he has returned from the brink of death, and if he can others may, but his words provoke despair because he has only returned to die: 'I am come/To bid my king and master aye good night.' Albany remembers what the audience have never forgotten, but there is a pause while the bodies of Goneril and Regan are brought on and then continuing confusion and delay:

Edmund.   Quickly send,
  Be brief in it, to th' castle; for my writ
  Is on the life of Lear and on Cordelia.
  Nay, send in time.
Albany.   Run, run! O, run!
Edgar.
  To who, my Lord? Who has the office? send
  Thy token of reprieve.
Edmund.
  Well thought on: take my sword,
  Give it the captain.
Edgar.   Haste thee, for thy life.
                                      (v, iii, 244–51)

Just when it seems Lear and Cordelia will be saved, the king makes his final entrance. John Reibetanz believes: 'Shakespeare has... prepared us for the play's final, pitiful tableau by associating Cordelia with Christ: the mortal result of "my father's business" was the best known fact of Renaissance spiritual life.'[1] I would have thought the best known fact of spiritual life was the resurrection rather than the crucifixion. Christianity depends upon the fact that the dead Christ in Mary's arms will rise again. I am not suggesting that Cordelia is a Christ-figure, merely that the tension created by the reversed Pieta stems from an emblem of death that contains a promise of rebirth. The audience are reminded of this when Lear says, if Cordelia lives 'It is a chance which does redeem all sorrows' (l. 266). Reibetanz locates many elements from Romance literature which relate *King Lear* to the Last Plays, and the possibility of a return to life, which is realised in those plays, is precisely the connection. Throughout the remainder of the scene, the possibility that Cordelia lives remains open and the audience continue to alternate between hope and despair. In this world of uncertainty, this is the greatest uncertainty of all. As I suggested earlier, Lear's speeches reveal a pattern of assertions, qualifications and contradictions (a familiar pattern in this play of reversed expectations) and this creates the audience's ambivalent response. Shakespeare's contemporaries must have wondered whether Cordelia would revive for a moment as Desdemona had done. In this play there are two precedents for a return to life: Gloucester's revival from a state resembling death,[2] and Kent's recovery from his trance.

The counter-argument is that Lear's confusion is not shared by the audience, because they do not view the scene through his eyes. However, the onlooker's comments provide little guidance. Kent and Edgar voice the audience's confusion: 'Is this the promis'd end?' 'Or image of that horror?' Albany is almost speechless: 'Fall and cease' and after this no one except Lear comments on Cordelia. During the dialogue between Kent and Lear, references to death accumulate: Lear 'kill'd the slave' who was hanging his daughter; Caius is 'dead and

[1] Reibetanz, *The Lear World*, p. 111.
[2] Notably Lear's awaking in the 'reconciliation scene' echoes Gloucester's words at Dover: *Gloucester.* 'Away, and let me die.' (IV, vi, 48); *Lear.* 'You do me wrong to take me out o' th' grave' (IV, vii, 45), so we might cite this as yet another precedent for a return to life.

rotten' (but no, he has returned from the grave as Kent); Goneril and Regan are dead and so is Edmund. At exactly the point where the spectators decide it is all over and Cordelia is dead, there is, as John Shaw suggests, a typical concluding speech. 'The wheel has come full circle' as Albany resigns the crown with an echo of Lear's opening words. The speech appears to move towards the concluding couplet:

> All friends shall taste
> The wages of their virtue, and all foes
> The cup of their deservings *bitter woes*[1]

but the couplet is broken: 'O! see, see!' and Lear delivers his final shattering speech with its unbearable, unanswerable, question: 'Why should a dog, a horse, a rat, have life,/And thou no breath at all?' (ll. 306–7). As I suggested in the beginning, again he moves from certainty to uncertainty, from despair to hope. For an audience who have been involved in a similar process, his death is a moment of absolute confusion. Even as they direct their attention to Cordelia, Lear falls. If for a second their hopes of life were reviving, this is the cruelest reversal in the play. Reibetanz believes they view 'Lear's final moments' 'through the steady eyes of Edgar', but the only steady eyes, as it turns out, belong to Kent. Edgar does not believe Lear is dead and his impulse is to hope for life: Kent on the contrary prays for death. The opposition is typical of the play. While the audience agree with Kent that Lear has suffered enough, they share Edgar's hopes and may even hear echoes of his words over Gloucester at Dover (the stage positions may complete the connection):

Edgar.   He faints! My Lord, my Lord!
Kent.
  Break, heart; I prithee, break!
Edgar.   Look up, my Lord.
Kent.
  Vex not his ghost: O! let him pass; he hates him
  That would on the rack of this tough world
  Stretch him out longer.   (v, iii, 311–15)

When Edgar decides 'He is gone, indeed' and Albany gives the order 'Bear them from hence', the audience are finally certain: it is finished. They are wrong. Shakespeare creates one last vivid image. Albany removes the crown from his head (this is Marvin Rosenberg's fine reading)[2] and says: 'Friends of my soul, you twain/Rule in this realm, and the gor'd state sustain.' Do Kent and Edgar stand each with a hand on the crown in a repetition of the moment in scene one (l. 139) when Albany and Cornwall did likewise? The play has demonstrated the terrible results of that first division of power and now there is a second. Or is there? Kent's final speech is usually played as his refusal of the crown (after all, he opposed the original division of power) and Edgar's speech is often a reluctant acceptance. There is a marked contrast between Kent's thoughts on death and Edgar's on youth, but the young man's words may imply he also refuses. The play ends as it began on a note of uncertainty:

Kent.
  I have a journey, sir, shortly to go;
  My master calls me, I must not say no.
Edgar.
  The weight of this sad time we must obey;
  Speak what we feel, not what we ought to say.
  The oldest hath borne most: we that are young
  Shall never see so much, nor live so long.

                              (v, iii, 321–6)

There is no emphasis on the restoration of order and no expressed hope in the future. On the contrary, the lines emphasise a general sense of diminution. With Lear's death something irreplaceable has gone out of the world and those who remain are smaller beings who can 'never see so much, nor live so long'. As the death march sounds, death finally holds dominion over all.

John Reibetanz believes: 'Edgar's desire to "Speak what we feel, not what we ought to

---

[1] John Shaw, '*King Lear:* The Final Lines', *Essays in Criticism*, 16 (1966), pp. 261–7, p. 264.
[2] Rosenberg, *The Masks of King Lear*, p. 322.

say"...shows that he has recognized the great value that resides in Cordelia's plainness, as opposed to her sisters' pleasing surfaces; and his words bring us to the same recognition.'[1] It would be remarkable if Edgar reached such a conclusion, since he has neither heard Cordelia speak nor occupied the stage with her until the final scene. The idea that any audience can sit back and respond with such 'clear-eyed moral insight and judgement'[2] strikes me as equally remarkable. Dr Johnson offers an excellent description of what happens at a performance of *King Lear* and it is ironic that he is describing the effect on a reader. The play, he says, 'fill[s] the mind with a perpetual tumult of indignation, pity, and hope...So powerful is the current of the poet's imagination that the mind which once ventures within it is hurried irresistibly along.'[3] The comment seems particularly applicable to the final scene, and it is this 'tumult' that precludes the affirmation for which some critics argue.

Bradley concluded that we realise 'our whole attitude in asking or expecting that goodness should be prosperous is wrong; that, if only we could see things as they are, we should see that the outward is nothing and the inward is all.'[4] Fine sentiments, but the audience can't 'see things as they are', can't even determine whether or not Cordelia lives, so how can they feel she is 'set free from life'?[5] For Bradley (and Reibetanz who follows him almost exactly) 'what happens to such a being does not matter; all that matters is what she is'.[6] This distinction is crucial to both critics' arguments, but it is one no spectator makes. For Bradley, Cordelia is 'a *thing* enskyed and sainted' (my emphasis),[7] but the dramatic structure Shakespeare creates ensures that the audience care intensely about what happens to her.

In an excellent essay, Nicholas Brooke accounts for the response of the affirming critics in terms of the kind of duality I've explored: 'Action and reaction are equal and opposite...

the sense of life in the presentation of death is the source of all this impulse to affirm.'[8] I would rather say 'the *possibility* of *continuing* life', because it is precisely because Shakespeare never takes up this possibility that some critics (like Tate before them) feel they must. As Brooke suggests: 'Hope springs eternal. It had better.'[9]

In the face of the uncertainty generated by the ending, it is natural to seek refuge in a dependable personal value, and it is because the play leaves the contraries unresolved that it forces us to look within ourselves and find there what we can. John Reibetanz believes '*King Lear* directs us to a realm of meaning that exists outside the *Lear* world'[10] and for him this meaning is Christian, but where the play directs us depends upon where we have the desire and the capacity to go. Shakespeare has left us with no single signpost. The play provokes a choice, but it makes none. However, while we may argue that the contraries remain unresolved and the questions unanswered, we should beware of suggesting that *King Lear* is, in our modern sense, 'open-ended'. Even Bradley admitted that pessimism is 'what we feel at times in reading'[11] and in performance this feeling is a great deal more pronounced because of the tension of uncertainty.

[1] Reibetanz, *The Lear World*, p. 121.
[2] Goldberg's comment on those who ignore the effects of performance and stress 'self-knowledge attained through suffering', p. 156.
[3] *Dr Johnson on Shakespeare*, ed. W. K. Wimsatt (Harmondsworth, 1969), p. 125.
[4] Bradley, *Shakespearean Tragedy*, p. 272.
[5] *Ibid.*, p. 270.
[6] *Ibid.*, pp. 271–2.
[7] *Ibid.*, p. 264.
[8] Nicholas Brooke, 'The Ending of *King Lear*', in *Shakespeare 1564–1964*, ed. E. A. Bloom (Providence, R. I., 1964), p. 87.
[9] *Ibid.*, p. 87.
[10] Reibetanz, *The Lear World*, p. 120.
[11] Bradley, *Shakespearean Tragedy*, p. 228.

© DEREK PEAT 1980

'KING LEAR' AND DOOMSDAY

MARY LASCELLES

There are numerous references to Doomsday (the Day of Judgement, the Last Day) in Shakespeare's plays. Many, at one end of the scale, amount to little more than casual profanity. Some, at the other, are (I believe) significant. By calling these *allusions*, I hope to designate their character and function. Allusion rests on analogy: it cites a correspondence, in respect of some property or attribute, between *this* and *that*. Like metaphor, it has no use for mere similarity: this is a correspondence rather between a pair of shoes than a pair of socks. It will, however, hardly speak home to the imaginative response of an audience if it is too abstruse or too personal: it touches the known, in an unfamiliar way. It should flatter the hearers' quickness of apprehension, not their patient ingenuity.

Somewhere between mere casual references and allusions heavily charged with significance come passages in which the correspondence between a particular situation and Doomsday denotes a measure of degree or extent. This can be bluntly paraphrased as 'I can't say worse than that, can I?' – or 'You can't see further than that, can you?' Thus, in 1 *Henry IV*, I, i, 29–30,[1] Winchester's tribute to the dead King –

> Unto the French the dreadful judgement-day
> So dreadful will not be as was his sight

– is a simple rhetorical figure measuring degree of dreadfulness. The Second Murderer's observation on the sleeping Clarence, 'Why, he shall never wake until the great judgement-day' (*Richard III*, I, iv, 104), though offered as a simple figure of extent – the furthest conceivable point in time – presently discovers unsuspected implications: a prospect of damnation.

A denser and more complex texture of allusion is discernible in Young Clifford's exclamation when he finds the dead body of his father:

> O, let the vile world end
> And the premised flames of the last day
> Knit earth and heaven together!
> Now let the general trumpet blow his blast...
>
> (2 *Henry VI*, v, ii, 40)

In his New Arden edition, 1957, A. S. Cairncross comments: 'A regular Shakespearean group of images, compounded from various sources, and centring on the Last Judgement, as presented in mediaeval art and thought. The situation is always one of horror aroused by the death of a dear friend or relative, and the effect on the bereaved that of chaos come again.' And he cites, as analogues, 'the great doom's image' in *Macbeth* and 'the promis'd end' in *Lear*. To this I should like to add that the context – Young Clifford's reflections on civil war – brings the passage markedly nearer to those in *Lear* and *Macbeth*, and that the emphasis on spectacle – flames and trumpet – fully justifies the reference to medieval *art*. On this account, I welcome A. S. Cairncross's

[1] References throughout to Peter Alexander's one-volume Shakespeare (London, 1951).

suggestion that *promis'd* in *Lear* might be emended to *premis'd*: the *premised end* being the end we have been taught to expect, taught, not only by precept but also by pictorial demonstration.

There remains, however, a wide divergence between these two Doomsday passages (in *Lear* and *Macbeth*) and every other Shakespearian reference to the event. In these alone the allusion is intrinsic, it chimes with tones which have been audible throughout either play. That the theme of judgement runs through *Macbeth* needs no demonstration. I hope to demonstrate that it is no less pervasive in *King Lear*. It is moreover my contention that, in order to understand this fully, we must consider the impact of certain pictorial representations of the Last Judgement on the imagination of those who formed Shakespeare's first audience. Furthermore, to recognise not only that this is a play burdened with a vision of Doomsday but also that its allusions to that vision were once able to recall a particular visual experience may help to explain impressions of waywardness made, here and there, upon a generation to which this experience is unknown.

I begin with objections which Edgar's course of action may prompt. From the outset, it defies probability – not, I admit, a major consideration in *King Lear*, but this instance of disregard for it deserves analysis. Edgar is first established by his own reaction to his brother's intrigue and that brother's characterisation of him, as simple almost to fatuity. But, on discovering his own predicament, he proposes to himself a stratagem requiring resource and cunning (II, iii); and on his next appearance embarks effortlessly on what will prove to be the first of a series of sophisticated impersonations: the Bedlam beggar – a virtuoso performance (III, iv). It is surely strange that he should sustain subsequent improvised parts with unflagging fertility of invention; even stranger that he, a man of indubitable good

will, should so employ this cunning as to drive the King further into insanity, and deprive his father of the only comfort he craves.

Disguise is so patent a convention on the stage, and so diverse in its uses – varying from the mere make-believe of masks (as in *Much Ado*) to effectual deception by means of stolen dress (as in *Cymbeline*) – that we should be able to accept the taking-off of clothes as equally effective with putting them on, for the concealment of identity. And, in an age when dress proclaimed a man's place in society, to be divested of it was to be signalised as an outcast from the social order of that age; if an outcast, a mendicant and probably a vagrant. Should it appear that a vagrant will best serve the dramatist's purpose, then we may assume that this purpose – here, surely, to meet a structural need of the play – governs the course undertaken and pursued by Edgar. Alike in play or novel,[1] a vagrant has one inalienable attribute: mobility. In Shakespearian practice, mobility is most often the Fool's contribution to a play's resilience. Feste, for example, passes unchallenged between one group of characters and another, altering his tone to suit each. I am not now referring to his deliberate impersonation, which will require attention presently, but only to his adaptability as he moves to and fro. This mobility is denied to Lear's Fool, by reason of his helpless dependence upon, and close attachment to, his master. Edgar, once he has established his disguise as impenetrable, enjoys the Fool's customary freedom of movement and association. But if this choice of role, the vagrant's, is thus far explicable, there remains one further question to be asked: why, among the diversity of vagrants generated by the disturbed economy of the times, this particular sort? Why the Bedlam beggar, the Abram man, poor Tom? This was a type familiar to readers of the popular vagabond

[1] Scott seems to have learnt from Shakespeare how to use this type for purposes not simply comic.

literature of the age;[1] all too familiar to frightened women in lonely farmhouses. Released from Bedlam with a licence to beg, he was by definition insane, and, according to the prevailing conception of insanity, possessed. Edgar describes the condition and behaviour of this particular type of social outcast in a soliloquy which gives him the whole stage and our undivided attention:

I . . . am bethought
To take the basest and most poorest shape
That ever penury in contempt of man
Brought near to beast . . .   (II, iii, 6–9)

He will deface his own image,

And with presented nakedness outface
The winds and persecutions of the sky.
The country gives me proof and precedent
Of Bedlam beggars, who, with roaring voices,
Strike in their numb'd and mortified bare arms
Pins, wooden pricks, nails, sprigs of rosemary;
And with this horrible object, from low farms,
Poor pelting villages, sheep-cotes, and mills,
Sometimes with lunatic bans, sometime with prayers,
Enforce their charity.   (II, iii, 11–20)

This is notably different from Kent's disguise, for which the livery of a rough serving-man and a moderate degree of self-caricature will suffice. It is, moreover, sharply distinguishable from Hamlet's 'antic disposition'. Again and again, Edgar makes it clear that he is assuming an established pattern of behaviour, from which he remains in himself wholly detached.

With the emergence of Edgar/Tom as the ostensibly possessed man in III, iv, it becomes evident that the devils which infest him have names and that these names would convey certain associations amongst Shakespeare's first audience. Nearly all of them, together with some of the phrases in which they are embedded, are to be found in Samuel Harsnet's *Declaration of Egregious Popish Impostures* (1603). This, it should be borne in mind, was Harsnet's second exercise in exposure of alleged possession and pretended exorcism.

It was Lewis Theobald who first drew attention to the correspondence between the names of devils in Harsnet's *Declaration* and *King Lear*. The influence of his discovery on editorial practice has been considerable. Malone's text is studded with notes on this or that particular correspondence; and from 1790[2] to the present editors have followed suit. In our day, Professor Muir has made the most thorough and systematic study of the parallel: first in an article, 'Samuel Harsnett and *King Lear*',[3] then in his edition of the play;[4] last, in his book *Shakespeare's Sources*.[5] Each of these amplifies its predecessor.

It was acute of Theobald to recognise that Shakespeare had used some of Harsnet's devil-names. It was, I believe, obtuse of him to call Harsnet's share of the *Declaration* 'a smart narrative', and to infer that Shakespeare was exploiting a contemporary scandal for the sake of its notoriety – but he cannot be held accountable for the consequences of his interpretation. It is strange that, far removed as we now are from his jovial scepticism, only one critic has (to my knowledge) asked the crucial question 'Why?'

Robert Stevenson's article, 'Shakespeare's Interest in Harsnett's *Declaration*'[6] gives cogent reasons for asking this question. There is, he argues, nothing in Shakespeare comparable with this full and exact recall of a piece of polemical theology. Other tracts on demonology would have served his purpose; why did he choose Harsnet? He proffers an answer, but it is one which raises difficulties of its own:

[1] See A. V. Judges, *The Elizabethan Underworld* (London, 1930), pp. 372–8.
[2] Johnson had mentioned the work casually when he suggested that IV, i, 59–63, lines absent from the folio, were omitted 'because I suppose the story was forgotten, the jest was lost'.
[3] *RES*, N.S. II (1951), 11–21.
[4] New Arden, 1952.
[5] London, 1957, vol. I.
[6] *PMLA*, LXVII (1952), 898–902.

among the Jesuits arraigned in this case some could have been personally known to Shakespeare. This would indeed account for his reading Harsnet's recital of it with close attention; but not, surely, for his making this very use of what he found there. A personal relationship, of whatever kind or degree, would hardly prompt a man to exhibit particulars of the charges in the framework of Edgar's grotesque impersonation.

Samuel Harsnet's[1] *Declaration of Egregious Popish Impostures* is composed of an account (narrative interspersed with denunciation) of a case which began in 1585, but dragged on into 1602 – this occupies 171 pages – together with examinations of witnesses and confessions of accused – a further 103 pages. The Jesuit 'Edmunds *alias* Weston', with a number of associates, was accused of inducing a sense of possession in certain persons, notably three maidservants, and proceeding to practise pretended exorcism on them. It appears that the bodies as well as the minds of the women were abused. This disgusting case is investigated without repugnance by a man who was to rise high under James I – regrettably, in the Church. Harsnet's cart-horse irony, his ostentatious learning, and that knowledge of the theatre which enabled him to present the affair in terms of play-acting, must have gained him enough readers to account for two further editions (1604 and 1605).

Before accepting unreservedly the position that Harsnet's *Declaration* is a major factor in the interpretation of *King Lear*, we should bring into focus for comparison his earlier (and in many ways similar) pamphlet: *A Discovery of the Fraudulent Practises of J. Darrel* (1599). Here he arraigned John Darrel, designated a Puritan, maintaining that he induced a youth, William Somers, with some others,[2] to feign possession, in order that he might seem to exorcise the evil spirit infesting them. As in the *Declaration*, such doings are likened to a theatrical performance: here, the reader is promised, in the prefatory Epistle, a 'puppet-show'. The matter and tone are indeed by so much the less distressing as the throes of the puppet are, than those of a living actor: the aim being exposure for the purpose of derision, not a criminal charge. It therefore seems likely that allusions to the *Discovery* should be carried by that mirthless jest, Feste's gulling of Malvolio under the pretence that he, as Sir Topas, is practising exorcism on the imprisoned 'madman'.[3]

The principal difference, however, between *Discovery* and *Declaration* is the virtual absence of devil-names from the earlier work. (One *Roofey* is mentioned, but there is nothing to match the legions called by name in the *Declaration*.)

In 1950, F. P. Wilson wrote: 'It is to be observed how little use he [Shakespeare] made in his plays of some of the books he looked at. We catch him dipping into that spirited piece of anti-Catholic propaganda, Samuel Harsnett's *Declaration of egregious Popish Impostures*, and coming up with the names of Edgar's fiends – Flibbertigibbet and the rest – and a few phrases.'[4] Would he have altered this if he had been able to revise the essay after the publication of Professor Muir's findings? Perhaps, but (I believe) not much. I suggest that we begin afresh, from this position – hypothetical, but not untenable: Shakespeare, wanting devils and devil-names, for a reason still to be determined, found his memory furnished with them. He had read the *Declaration* through –

[1] Harsnet on both title-pages (and of course in S.T.C.). Elsewhere (except in Peter Alexander's *Shakespeare*, 1964) Harsnett.

[2] Will Somers's case occupies 264 pages, the rest are summarily dismissed in the remaining 60.

[3] See, for example, introduction by Morton Luce to the 1937 Arden edition of *Twelfth Night*, p. xxi.

[4] 'Shakespeare's Reading', first printed in *Shakespeare Survey 3* (Cambridge, 1950); reprinted posthumously in *Shakespearian and Other Studies* (Oxford, 1969), p. 136.

Robert Stevenson's explanation is the only one hitherto advanced – and remembered, or perhaps found himself unable to forget, some of the names contained in it. Has the process by which names are lodged in the memory been sufficiently considered? Unprecedented and outlandish names are explored *as though* by the tongue. It is not necessarily a pleasurable experience, any more than the exploration of a decaying tooth is pleasurable; but it can, like that, be compulsive. I do not question Theobald's characterisation of the *Declaration* as 'this popular piece of satire'.[1] I do call in question any inference which supposes Shakespeare to have exploited this satire, and to that end foisted Harsnet's devils into his play. I am therefore obliged to offer an alternative explanation for what G. S. Gordon calls the demon-haunted world of *Lear*.[2]

The source of that emotional response upon which this and kindred suggestions work, in this play, is fear; and it is a fear whose onset is sudden. Whereas *Hamlet* and many of the histories had opened in a mood of foreboding, the ostensible occasion of the opening of *Lear* is as festive as a royal birthday. The King's own mood, for all his talk of age and death, is overweening self-confidence, and confidence in the willingness of others to play out the play according to his design. Only knowledge of the story tells us that his assurance is misplaced; and we have no such reason for distrusting Gloucester's complacency. Hence we have to be *precipitated* into fear; and – unlike the apprehension and despondency of Leir and Perillus in the old play – this pervasive fear exceeds altogether the sum of its circumstantial causes.

Fear is a passion which, more powerfully than any other, works upon us by evocation: it obeys the prompting of allusion rather than statement. The disproportion between cause and effect cannot be explained in rational terms. Lear on the heath is suffering more than the anguish of outraged fatherhood – the storm within. Those who are apprehensive on his account fear something more than the exposure of an old man to the storm without. All this we must be brought to understand with uncommon rapidity. Between the glib references of Regan and Cornwall to the inconvenience of remaining out of doors on such a night, and Cordelia's heart-broken lament for the harm it has done her father,[3] something has happened to Lear which transcends the event and even her compassionate understanding – and it goes on happening, to the end. Critics (always so much more moral than Shakespeare, as Walter Raleigh pointed out) affirm that Lear has come to a sense of his own misdoing. How then should his experience penetrate us? – *as it does*. We have not all lost a kingdom through our own fault, nor even wronged a daughter. How is this deep perturbation evoked in us? How was it evoked in that first audience?

It is to the second of these questions that (I believe) a circumstantial answer can be offered. Too much emphasis has been laid, in the interpretation of this play, on verbal allusions. I propose, as I have intimated, to consider a visual allusion: the Doomsday paintings, especially those over the chancel arch in so many English churches.[4] Superseding the more allusive, earlier representations of Christ in Majesty, these Dooms established in the late fourteenth and early fifteenth centuries, what may be called a stereotype – determined (I sup-

[1] *The Works of Shakespeare* (London, 1733), v, 164.
[2] 'A Note on the World of *King Lear*' in *Shakespearian Comedy and Other Studies* (Oxford, 1944), pp. 116–28. [3] II, iv, 303–6; IV, vii, 30–42.
[4] See A. Caiger-Smith, *English Mediaeval Mural Paintings* (Oxford, 1963); M. D. Anderson, *History and Imagery in British Churches* (1971). 'Except for the image of St. Christopher, the Judgement was by far the most frequent of the themes of wall-paintings; it almost always occupied the most arresting position in churches, the space over the chancel arch' (Caiger-Smith, p. 31, where seventy-eight are enumerated). More are still being uncovered – e.g., Kidlington.

pose) in part by the space allotted them. They were explicit, even to crudity; and, taking into account this characteristic and the resemblance among them, we may perhaps liken them to posters, which, reproduced and displayed in many places, can be resented but not easily forgotten. They must, in the fifteenth and early sixteenth centuries, have been familiar to numberless church-goers. But how many of them survived the first phase of Tudor iconoclasm, and the subsequent sporadic 'defacement of images'?

To this question of survival, I can reply only with an estimate of probability.[1] It should, in the first place, be remembered that the opprobrious term 'images' included statues, wall-paintings, and the embellishment of shrines. Of these, the paintings were least likely to give offence, being seldom if ever associated with superstitious practices or claims to miraculous effects; and Doomsday paintings – subject to one provision – would not be obnoxious to a sixteenth-century congregation, however they may affect us. St Michael might be shown weighing souls, provided there were no intercession on behalf of any soul in the scales.[2]

Although information available to visitors in parish churches can tell when these paintings were first discovered – and sometimes covered again, so horrifying were their implications – it seems impossible to ascertain when they had first been covered with lime-wash; and it is doubtful whether access to original records would yield certainty. The chapel of the Trinity in Stratford-upon-Avon is a case in point. It belonged to the Guild of the Holy Cross; and, since it is variously named in references, it will be convenient to call it the Guild Chapel. The tremendous Doomsday painting over its chancel arch was first released from its obliterating, and protective, coat of lime-wash in 1804. Thomas Fisher, the antiquary, made drawings of this and the paintings on the walls of the

nave, which were published with a descriptive account by John Gough Nichols in 1838.[3] These drawings, as reproduced by lithography, are crude but clear and vigorous. The paintings were then covered afresh. When they were once more uncovered, E. W. Tristram made a drawing of the Doom[4] – now much fainter – which illustrates the artistic merit he claims for it. Unfortunately, the belief that it must have been familiar to Shakespeare[5] was shaken by the entry in the Chamberlains' Accounts for 1562–3: 'Item payd for defaysing Ymages in yᵉ chappell ijs.'[6] The man charged with this operation was John Shakespeare. It is therefore a generally-accepted view that this Doom was covered with lime-wash before John's son William was born.

Nevertheless, I would regard the obliteration of the Stratford Doom in 1562–3 as probable rather than proven: urging that 'images' is a term of diverse connotations at that date; and that, even supposing it to have signified mural paintings in this entry, those on the walls of the nave were far more likely to provoke

[1] See Caiger-Smith, *English Medieval Mural Paintings*, chapter VIII, 'The Destruction of Images'.

[2] This transaction was obliterated from the Doomsday painting at Penn in Buckinghamshire. See Caiger-Smith, *ibid.*, p. 35.

[3] Thomas Fisher and John Gough Nichols, *Ancient Allegorical, Historical and Legendary Paintings on the walls of the chapel of the Trinity, belonging to the Gilde of the Holy Cross at Stratford-upon-Avon in Warwickshire* (London, 1838). Fisher had returned for a further inspection in 1807.

[4] Published with a descriptive account in *The Illustrated London News*, 27 April 1929. The original drawing is in the Victoria and Albert Museum. There is also an article in *The Burlington Magazine*, May 1930, by E. T. Long, 'Some Recently Discovered English Wall Paintings'.

[5] Lionel Cust, in *Shakespeare's England* (Oxford, 1916), II, 4.

[6] *Minutes and Accounts of the Corporation and Other Records*, ed. R. Savage and E. Fripp, Publications of the Dugdale Society (Stratford-upon-Avon, 1921–9), I, 128. Cited by E. K. Chambers, *William Shakespeare* (Oxford, 1930), I, 9.

iconoclasm, including as they did the death of Thomas à Becket and the Finding of the True Cross. They were besides more easily accessible than that over the chancel arch. They are now in worse case. Even should these arguments be disallowed in respect of the Stratford Doom, there remains the very strong probability that many other Doomsday paintings of this type had survived into the second half of the sixteenth century: the Puritans of that time complained that iconoclasm was half-hearted and white-wash insufficient to conceal wall-paintings; and enough 'images' seem to have been left to occupy the zeal of their successors under the Commonwealth.[1]

The similarity among these Dooms, conditioned as they were by the space available,[2] allows a generic description to be offered. The design is vertical, there is no near and far, only higher and lower. In the apex of the arch, Christ sits in judgement. Around and below him are ranged angels, apostles, saints; close to his knees often appear the Virgin Mary and St John – usually the Evangelist, but sometimes (as at Stratford – see Plate v) the Baptist.[3] In the lowest part of the painting the figures shown in motion are sharply divided: on the Judge's right hand – that is, to the left of the picture as we see it – the blessed are conducted towards a heavenly gate, at which St Peter usually receives them; on our right (and it will be convenient to continue the description in these terms) the lost are driven or drawn into the mouth of hell, marshalled by fiends; a little lower, on this side, they are tormented. These are not the only figures to occupy the lowest parts of the painting; there are also souls emerging from their graves, and looking upwards. I say *parts* because the left and right of its lowest level are separated by the aperture of the arch; and this causes a sort of imbalance in the distribution of the graves: since the blessed are in an ascending and the lost in a descending train, there is more room at the left than at the

right foot of the picture, and this is usually filled by graves and emerging figures. One particular should be borne in mind, because it is an almost constant[4] visual impression: the nakedness of all these souls, both those awaiting judgement and those who have been judged. As an indication of their state, this is not remarkable; but it does heighten the terror and pity of their predicament.[5]

The dominant theme of these paintings is that account of the Judgement propounded in the Athanasian Creed: 'At whose coming all men shall rise again with their bodies and shall give account for their own works. And they that have done good shall go into life everlasting and they that have done evil into everlasting fire.' It is, however, given an extension of meaning by the message of St Matthew's Gospel, chapters 24 and 25 – especially 25 – as both the authorities I have already cited affirm:[6] 'Inasmuch as ye have done it unto one of the least of these my brethren, ye have done it unto me' (25.40) – with its terrible complement: 'Then shall he answer them, saying, Verily I say unto you, Inasmuch as ye did it not to one of the least of these, ye did it not to me' (25.45).

[1] Caiger-Smith, *English Medieval Mural Paintings*, pp. 113, 115–16.
[2] The spring of the arch, and the pitch of the roof, varying from church to church, may influence arrangement; and perhaps the craftsman sometimes found the space they allowed insufficient for his needs: at South Leigh the picture has spread on to adjacent walls.
[3] See E. W. Tristram, *English Wall Painting in the Fourteenth Century*, ed. Eileen Tristram (London, 1955), p. 19.
[4] The wall-paintings at Chalgrove seem to be the only representation of souls emerging fully clothed from their graves. In the Doom over the chancel arch in St Thomas's Church, Salisbury, the dishonest ale-wife alone is clothed – an anomalous comic figure.
[5] At Cliffe-at-Hoo the blessed retain vestiges of grave-clothes, as do figures emerging from graves in some paintings.
[6] Caiger-Smith, *English Medieval Mural Paintings*, pp. 6–7 and 31; Anderson, *History and Imagery in British Churches*, pp. 115, 125 and 145.

It should be evident that, in these Doomsday paintings, the part most visible to the congregation, indeed, inescapable, was the lowest area: that which showed bodies – naked or with vestiges of shrouds – emerging from graves, and naked bodies herded together and driven into hell. Moreover, this latter subject invited a dreadful inventiveness on the part of the craftsman, in the representation of fiends and their activities. If this was, as I believe, a familiar spectacle, it must have been hard to forget.

There would thus be at Shakespeare's disposal, when he needed to evoke overmastering fear, a common visual experience readily recalled by allusion. The dominant impression in this visual pattern is nakedness – signifying defencelessness, but with a further suggestion of suddenly-realised equality. Emblematic head-dress – crown or mitre – suggests a former differentiation, now meaningless.

Among Elizabethan vagrants, the Bedlam beggar seems to have been marked out by his nearly naked plight; and it is clear that Edgar as originally played presented this condition, so far as stage decency allowed. This, I surmise, prompts the Fool's insistence that the strange figure lurking in the hovel is a *spirit* (III, iv, 39 and 42). It certainly gives point to Lear's question, when he supposes Poor Tom to have been reduced to this state by his daughters – 'Could'st thou save nothing? Would'st thou give them all?' – with the Fool's rejoinder, 'Nay, he reserv'd a blanket, else we had all been sham'd' (63–5). This particular will recur, with curious insistence, not only in Lear's 'Thou wert better in a grave than to answer with thy uncover'd body the extremity of the skies' (100–3), but also in Gloucester's recollection of 'the naked fellow' (IV, i, 41 and 50), and his plea to the Old Man: 'Bring some covering for this naked soul' (*ibid.*, 45).

And so the ambiguous figure of the Bedlam beggar, sufferer or sinner or both, victim or impostor, with his 'presented nakedness' and his infestation by fiends, has much in common with those beings in Doomsday paintings. United thus, the two images wake a deep and powerful fear. Lear, who will be drawn into the world of Tom's fiend-haunted imagination, has himself projected the theme of nakedness, with its concomitant equality, into *our* imagination in a strange and sudden way. Left to his own thoughts outside the hovel, he has uttered that memorable invocation:

Poor naked wretches, wheresoe'er you are,
That bide the pelting of this pitiless storm,
How shall your houseless heads and unfed sides,
Your loop'd and window'd raggedness, defend
    you
From seasons such as these? O, I have ta'en
Too little care of this!   (III, iv, 28–33)

and he proceeds to the medieval doctrine, itself familiar from exposition in wall-paintings, that the poor man is the direct responsibility of the man who has it in his power to relieve him.[1] Edwin Muir and Professor L. C. Knights have both argued persuasively[2] that the play expresses a conflict between the old, time-honoured pieties and loyalties and a new policy of ruthelss self-advancement. Certainly Lear, for all his impulsive errors, pays heartfelt if incomplete tribute to an older, more stable order in terms of

The offices of nature, bond of childhood,
Effects of courtesy, dues of gratitude...

        (II, iv, 177–8)

[1] E.g., in the Works of Mercy and Seven Deadly Sins at Trotton (Anderson, *History and Imagery in British Churches*, Plate 46) the souls of the man who has relieved want, and the man who has denied help, are shown naked at the Judgement Seat; thereafter, the just man is clothed, and the niggard naked and tormented. See also G. R. Owst, *Literature and Pulpit in Mediaeval England* (Oxford, 1966), pp. 560–2.

[2] Edwin Muir, *The Politics of 'King Lear'*, W. P. Ker Lecture for 1946 reprinted in *Essays on Literature and Society* (London, 1949); L. C. Knights, *Shakespeare's Politics: with some Reflections on the Nature of Tradition*, Annual Shakespeare Lecture of the British Academy for 1957.

And all the well-disposed characters subscribe, each in his own way; the Fool, by his bitter insistence that it is Lear himself who has untied these bonds and let loose disorder.

Lear's vision, contemplated in its entirety – and this will not be easy – must surely lie very close to the meaning of the play. In such Judgement plays as survive among the Guild cycles,[1] the kings and other potentates may be regarded as spokesmen for the assembled souls. Lear is evidently much more than this. 'Bad'[2] kings in the Guild plays confess to a bewildering variety of sins – debasing the currency, for example – as they move towards a culmination clearly intended to recall Matthew 25. Lear's self-arraignment follows a course which, despite the vagaries of madness, seems to be charged, perhaps over-charged, with a meaning integral to the play.

The first intimation of Lear's preoccupation with Judgement comes with the rising storm: he calls on the gods, whom he still regards as allies, to make this an occasion of Judgement by disclosing undivulged guilt (III, ii, 49–59). I avoid the term Judgement Day on account of its conventional associations, although, in a Britain where floods may threaten *steeples* and *weathercocks*, anachronistic references to Christian usage matter very little. There is nothing to perplex, and therefore nothing to require specific comment, in the likening of the thunder to 'dreadful summoners'; but neither is there any reason why this metaphor should not recall the angelic summons, by trumpet or other wind instrument, shown in all the paintings. (It is part of the horror of these representations that the devils are allowed to join in with their horns.)

It is while Lear is still fighting to retain his sanity that he invokes those 'poor naked wretches' whose misery is a rebuke to him (III, iv, 28–37). I must ask leave to defer consideration of this passage and its relevance to

my argument until that, in its course, reaches the point of his return to sanity.

In his madness, Lear is obsessed with ideas of human justice. He passes from a doubt of its sufficiency to a conviction of its impossibility. The first impulse, the mock trial of his daughters (III, vi, 20, *passim* to 78), is a direct reaction to his own situation. But whereas, on reverting to the theme of human justice in IV, vi, he is still in the judgement-seat – 'I pardon that man's life' (109) – he is coming to question the worth of pardon or validity of sentence. From social satire such as can be found in many sorts of contemporary literature he passes to these images: the figure on the bench which might well change places with that in the dock, the farmer's dog in authority, the big and little plunderers of their fellows – and so to the idea of Justice itself as an imposture, concealing our common guilt. Therefore he will himself override this perverted justice with a gesture of amnesty. The underlying despair of 'None does offend, none, I say, none' (168) is a world away from Cymbeline's easy 'Pardon's the word to all' (v, v, 422). It is the distance between tragi-comedy and tragedy.

Although these judgement fantasies of Lear's madness are interspersed with references to hell and devils, they imply no appeal to, nor shrinking from, any concept of divine Justice.

Before returning to Lear's last sane utterance, and considering its relation to the words which will mark his restoration to sanity (IV, vii, 45–9), I find myself obliged to offer a personal impression, which is (of course) quite insignificant – unless it prompts others to look at the object and note their own reactions to it. In the English mural-paintings I have seen, the souls rising from graves and the souls consigned to hell form a conspicuous part of the most

[1] E.g., York, Chester, the incomplete Towneley and the fragmentary *Ludus Coventriae*.

[2] All have sinned; these have sought mercy tardily and ineffectually.

clearly visible portion of the composition; they are nearly all facing towards us, and I can see in their faces hardly any intimation of the painter's wish to signalise evil.[1] Yet there were established conventions for depicting the faces not only of devils but also of human adversaries of the saints. Among possible explanations, I suggest one which must rest on an appeal to common experience. According to Matthew 25.45, they stand convicted of the sin of omission; and sins of omission are those that most trouble the conscience: opportunities for them are far more numerous, and they make less immediate impact on the consciousness. This does not mean that the look of simple dismay on the faces in these paintings – so different from the expressions of the lost in the Judgements of great masters[2] – is meant to extenuate the guilt of those who, in denying human need, have denied Christ: nothing so unedifying. Rather is it intended to convey the truth that this is our common predicament.

This may help us to understand something which is surely surprising, certainly precipitate, in Lear's cry to the poor naked wretches: still in command of his thoughts, he is himself facing judgement – the challenge of his own former life as ruler. But, suppose he were answering in this capacity Malcolm's interrogatory, how many of the 'king-becoming graces' (*Macbeth*, IV, iii, 91–4) would he be able to claim? Justice, temperance, lowliness, patience? Why should he so promptly single out care of the poor as the obligation in which he has come short? Solely because he is himself now destitute, or for a deeper cause, one which touches us all as this threat of reversal cannot? It may have been the intention of the Guild plays to bring this sin of omission home to everyone through the verdict on the bad ruler; but, even granted the benefit of better texts than we possess, the exigencies of stage presentation would forbid it. The souls cannot be shown rising from their graves[3] – we miss the

impact of an awakening: the full recognition of a truth long known but never accepted. This surely was what gave point, in those minds familiar with the Doom paintings, to Lear's forlorn admission:

> O, I have ta'en
> Too little care of this!

There remain two more significant allusions, on my reckoning, to be considered. When Lear comes to himself, in all the agony this entails, he expostulates with those who stand round: 'You do me wrong to take me out o' th' grave' (IV, vii, 45), and then singles out Cordelia: 'Thou art a soul in bliss.' It is to the saints ranged above them that the souls who rise from their graves in the Doom paintings look up, and sometimes stretch their arms. That Lear continues

> but I am bound
> Upon a wheel of fire, that mine own tears
> Do scald like molten lead –

and that no wheel of fire appears, among the torments of hell, in any chancel painting that I have seen or heard of, is of small consequence. Literary analogues have been proposed by editors; and a common cut, used in *The Kalender of Shepherdes*,[4] shows the torture of the wheel as punishment of pride. But the correspondence seems to me neither close[5] nor necessary. The image has surely been conceived expressly for its purpose, to convey poignantly Lear's conviction that what he has done separates him for ever from Cordelia. Furthermore, if the

[1] Very seldom a single figure standing apart, like the ale-wife of Salisbury, shows a different intention.

[2] See for example Robert Hughes, *Heaven and Hell in Western Art* (London, 1968).

[3] In the York Judgement, there are explicit references to a reunion of soul and body which has taken place elsewhere.

[4] *The Kalender of Shepherdes*, ed. H. O. Sommer (London, 1892). The cut here reproduced, on p. 68, illustrates the account given by Lazarus of the pains of hell as revealed to him by death.

[5] There are no souls in bliss, for this is hell.

whole passage once derived some of its power from the evocation of a familiar visual experience, the sight of a Doomsday painting over a chancel arch, then the Folio reading for Lear's next question –

You are a spirit, I know. Where did you die? –

becomes at once clear and appropriate, these pictures representing, not any particular place, but the whole globe revealed as a graveyard at the Last Day. The souls depicted stand as tokens for all those assembled in an instant – as Donne was to represent them:

> At the round world's imagin'd corners, blow
> Your trumpets, Angells, and arise, arise
> From death, you numberlesse infinities
> Of soules, and to your scattred bodies goe...[1]

In such a context, it is natural enough to ask: Where did you die?

Last of all, there is the explicit, but still enigmatic, allusion to a pictured Doomsday, in that response of Albany, Kent and Edgar to the sight of Lear with Cordelia dead in his arms:

> *Kent.*   Is this the promis'd end?
> *Edgar.*
>   Or image of that horror?   (v, iii, 263–4)

This promised – or, as I would prefer to suppose, premised – end, with Albany's ensuing prayer for a termination, can refer only to Doomsday. Not, however, as a purely intellectual concept. Regarded so, the exchange between Kent and Edgar would fall into anticlimax – as though one should say (for example) 'Is this Armageddon, or merely a spectacle intended to represent it?' Admittedly, the order in which choric utterances are delivered need not be logical; but these lines establish themselves as choric mainly because we recognise them as allusive, their allusion framed to evoke traditional recollections: that inescapable consciousness of *the thing seen* which I have here tried to reconstruct.

[1] John Donne, *The Divine Poems*, ed. Helen Gardner (Oxford, 1952), p. 8.

I acknowledge gratefully suggestions from Mr and Mrs Emrys Jones.

LEAR'S LAST SPEECH

BY

J. K. WALTON

The suggestion that Lear dies from an unbearable joy induced by the belief that Cordelia is alive was first put forward by A. C. Bradley,[1] and has been adopted by some subsequent critics.[2] It deserves perhaps a fuller consideration than it is usually given.[3] The point, after all, is not a small one. If he dies from joy thinking that Cordelia still lives he dies, unlike all other tragic heroes, not aware that any tragedy has taken place, for the other deaths are not to be thought of as tragic. Nor is the problem one which can be considered independently of an interpretation of the play as a whole. The question of Lear's final consciousness is clearly part of the larger question of the interpretation to be given to the general theme of ignorance and knowledge which has an important role throughout the drama. I hope to show that an analysis of the various stages and forms which this theme takes helps in the interpretation of Lear's last speech.

A recurring situation throughout the play is that of a belief, assumption, or hope which is quickly shown to be false by the impact of events. Lear is at first repeatedly made to acquire knowledge in this manner, and since he rejects the advice of Kent, it is the sole means by which he is able to learn. The process by which he acquires knowledge—his treatment by Goneril, his discovery that fifty of his followers have been dismissed, his finding Kent in the stocks, and his reception by Regan—is brought into all the clearer focus since at this stage he is alone in learning by this method. It is only later, from near the end of Act III onwards, that other characters are subjected to a similar process. We should, however, remember that while in the first two acts Lear is suffering continuously, he is not a passive character in a physical sense. To a considerable extent he has physically the initiative. He gives away his kingdom, rejects Cordelia, and banishes Kent. He could, if he wished, have submitted to Goneril's demands, but instead he chooses to go to Regan. His decision to go into the storm is his own; here again he could have capitulated. Nor is he passive in the storm. He contends 'with the fretful elements', and 'Strives in his little world of man to out-storm / The to-and-fro-conflicting wind and rain' (III, i, 4 ff.). But during the storm the nature of his initiative changes. Hitherto his initiative has consisted in various deeds. His mind, at least in its acquisition of knowledge, has been more acted upon than acting. During the storm he loses initiative so far as action is concerned, but his mind ceases to be passive in regard to learning. The active role of his mind, which with an awakened imaginative sympathy now begins to generalize his own experience, is first displayed[4] when he shows pity for the Fool (III, ii, 68), and declares that

> The art of our necessities is strange,
> And can make vile things precious.[5]　　　　　　　　　　　(III, ii, 70–1)

Formerly his utterances (apart from his talk with the Fool) have consisted mainly of orders, denunciations of others, or appeals to the heavens.

From now on Lear's capacity to acquire knowledge goes together with an ability to perceive the sufferings of others. The prayer 'Poor naked wretches...' (III, iv, 28 ff.), which he utters on his next appearance, is based on his recognition of the existence of 'houseless heads and unfed sides', with their 'loop'd and window'd raggedness', of which earlier he has taken 'Too little care'. The arrival of Edgar disguised as mad Tom—which is the last of the blows which Lear is to receive in the first stage of his education and that which causes him on one level to lose his sanity—is also the one which decisively sets his mind on its quest of knowledge. Henceforth he progresses not only from having knowledge inflicted on him to a capacity for summing up the implications of his experience; he also actively seeks knowledge out by the use of 'reason in madness'. He sees Edgar as the image of truth—'unaccommodated man is no more but such a poor, bare, forked animal as thou art' (III, iv, 109–11)—and proceeds to tear off his own clothes in an action expressive of his desire to find reality. His quest for truth is carried further by his questionings of Edgar, who from being the image of truth has now become its source:

> First let me talk with this philosopher.
> What is the cause of thunder? (III, iv, 158–9)

and he declares that 'I'll talk a word with this same learned Theban' (l. 161), and 'I will keep still with my philosopher' (l. 180).

The 'trial' of Goneril and Regan, which takes place when Lear next appears (III, vi), represents an extension of his newly acquired attitude of mind. He is no longer content merely to denounce; he wants an investigation into the matter which will weigh the evidence and judicially establish its finding. But the justice which he imagines does not work. Goneril, whom he has arraigned, escapes and he perceives corruption in the 'False justicer'. He continues the inquisition with a medical rather than a judicial image in his mind. Almost his last words in the storm scenes are, 'let them anatomize Regan, see what breeds about her heart. Is there any cause in nature that makes these hard hearts?' (III, vi, 80–81).

Lear's search for knowledge has not yet been able to achieve a resolution. In the account of him which Kent is given in IV, iii, we hear that the condition of his mind prevents him from meeting Cordelia:

> A sovereign shame so elbows him: his own unkindness,
> That stripp'd her from his benediction, turn'd her
> To foreign casualties, gave her dear rights
> To his dog-hearted daughters, these things sting
> His mind so venomously that burning shame
> Detains him from Cordelia. (IV, iii, 43–8)

The next development of Lear's capacity for acquiring knowledge occurs when he meets Gloucester (IV, vi). The last time we saw Lear he had attempted to obtain justice, but he had sensed its inadequacy. In this scene he is able to proceed to an analysis of justice and authority which includes in its scope his own exercise of them in the initial action of the play. He can now summarize all that he has already learned, and develop his knowledge still further. His mind is recalled to what he once was, in fact as well as in name, by Gloucester's 'Is't not the King?' (l. 110). Lear's imagination is now able to comprehend both the authority he had as King and the knowledge which he has gained by his decision to abandon that authority. His full expression of this knowledge does not come at once. The way is, however, prepared for it by his answer to Gloucester:

> Ay, every inch a king:
> When I do stare, see how the subject quakes.
> I pardon that man's life. What was thy cause?
> Adultery?
> Thou shalt not die: die for adultery! No:
> The wren goes to't, and the small gilded fly
> Does lecher in my sight.   (IV, vi, 110–16)

The thought is already present, if only as yet indirectly expressed, that none offends because everyone offends, especially those who are most ostentatious in their virtue ('yond simp'ring dame'). What generates Lear's final development of the knowledge he has gained is, appropriately, the continued presence of Gloucester who, on a lower level, has had an experience similar to his own.[6] Prompted by Gloucester's physical blindness—'A man may see how this world goes with no eyes' (ll. 151–2)—Lear makes his culminating analysis of the reality that underlies the appearance of things:

> Look with thine ears: see how yond justice rails upon yond simple thief. Hark, in thine ear: change places, and, handy-dandy, which is the justice, which is the thief? Thou hast seen a farmer's dog bark at a beggar?
>
> *Glou.* Ay, Sir.
>
> *Lear.* And the creature run from the cur? There thou might'st behold
> The great image of Authority:
> A dog's obey'd in office.
> Thou rascal beadle, hold thy bloody hand!
> Why dost thou lash that whore? Strip thine own back;
> Thou hotly lusts to use her in that kind
> For which thou whipp'st her. The usurer hangs the cozener.
> Thorough tatter'd clothes small vices do appear;
> Robes and furr'd gowns hide all. Plate sin with gold,
> And the strong lance of justice hurtless breaks;
> Arm it in rags, a pigmy's straw does pierce it.
> None does offend, none, I say, none; I'll able 'em:
> Take that of me, my friend, who have the power
> To seal th'accuser's lips.   (IV, vi, 152–72)

The conclusion is that there can be no real justice in a society where inequality of conditions exists. Lear himself had been a victim even while he had exercised authority. He has earlier told how he was blinded by flattery—'They flattered me like a dog...they told me I was every thing'—and how he did not find them out until 'the thunder would not peace at my bidding' (ll. 97 ff.). The conclusion 'None does offend, none, I say, none' follows from his newly won knowledge. He ceases to demand that justice be executed on Goneril and Regan. He is now ready to be freed from the conflict in his mind which arises from the co-existence of a desire for punishment for those who have injured him and a feeling that he himself is guilty. This is not to say that when his meeting with Cordelia takes place he does not feel guilty. He is 'bound / Upon a wheel of fire' (IV, vii, 46–7), and he tells her 'If you have poison for me, I will drink it' (l. 72). But his mind is now in a condition in which he is capable of receiving her forgiveness. The sleep from which he wakes is the immediate cause of his restored sanity, but we impoverish the play if we see him on regaining his wits as merely enfeebled by what he has been through. He describes himself, admittedly, as 'a very foolish fond old man' (l. 60), but it is a necessary part of his present greatness that he should be able to see himself in this light. His simplicity is the result not so much of weakness as of the resolution of tension which he himself, through his pursuit of knowledge, has achieved. His thought has been raised to a higher level by his struggles, a level which includes, unalloyed with madness, the knowledge he has gained.

Lear's newly developed strength is shown as soon as he is once more exposed to adversity. When he and Cordelia are captured, she asks 'Shall we not see these daughters and these sisters?', and he replies:

> No, no, no, no! Come, let's away to prison;
> We two alone will sing like birds i' th' cage:
> When thou dost ask me blessing, I'll kneel down,
> And ask of thee forgiveness: so we'll live,
> And pray, and sing, and tell old tales, and laugh
> At gilded butterflies, and hear poor rogues
> Talk of court news; and we'll talk with them too,
> Who loses and who wins; who's in, who's out;
> And take upon's the mystery of things,
> As if we were Gods' spies: and we'll wear out,
> In a wall'd prison, packs and sects of great ones
> That ebb and flow by th'moon.   (v, iii, 8–19)

We must not, like Bradley,[7] think of this speech as showing Lear's pathetic blindness to his position now that he and Cordelia are prisoners, and as an actual plan, soon to be rendered impossible, of how he is to spend the remainder of his old age. That he is not speaking literally is shown by the declaration that 'we'll wear out, / In a wall'd prison, packs and sects of great ones / That ebb and flow by th'moon'. Lear has always been conscious of his age, and he can hardly be here taken as actually expecting a further long lease of life. His mind is now raised far above the immediate events by which he is assailed, because of the knowledge he has acquired, a knowledge that enables him to evaluate the 'packs and sects of great ones' at their true worth. What unites him for ever to Cordelia is their active interest in truth: they will 'take upon's the mystery of things, / As if we were Gods' spies'. The difference between the old and the new Lear is further emphasized in his next speech when he says, 'The good years shall devour them, flesh and fell, / Ere they shall make us weep' (ll. 24–5). These words recall his blustering threats to Goneril just before he goes into the storm, when he speaks of the terrors he shall inflict on her before he will weep (II, iv, 280 ff.). Here, however, he is not making an empty threat but a prophecy, for when he does next weep Goneril and Regan are in fact both dead.[8]

70

We have seen how, until a change takes place in the storm, Lear has been forced to acquire knowledge through the impact of events, and how during this period he is alone in so acquiring it. But at the same time as Lear is changing from one on whom knowledge is inflicted to one who seeks it out, other characters begin to have to learn in the way he had to learn, by being subjected to sudden blows which destroy their illusions and hopes. The first to undergo this form of education is Cornwall and, ironically, the lesson is administered by one of the humble, a recognition of whose existence has been the earliest sign of Lear's awakened and now active mind. When the servant takes Cornwall to task for blinding Gloucester, he exclaims incredulously 'My villain!' (III, vii, 77), and he is echoed by Regan's 'A peasant stand up thus!' (l. 79). For Cornwall 'Untimely comes this hurt' (l. 97). It is almost immediately after Cornwall has been attacked that Gloucester learns from Regan that it was Edmund who betrayed him. An experience similar to Cornwall's awaits Oswald when he jubilantly exclaims on seeing Gloucester,

> Most happy!
> That eyeless head of thine was first fram'd flesh
> To raise my fortunes. (IV, vi, 227–9)

He too is incredulous at being withstood by one of apparently base degree ('Slave, thou hast slain me'), and dies exclaiming 'O! untimely death' (l. 252).

Like Cornwall and Oswald, the other evil characters experience a swift overtaking by events. Regan is struck untimely down by her sister's poison just when she hopes to gain Edmund. Goneril herself displays, by the inadequacy of her remark on Edmund's overthrow ('thou art not vanquish'd, / But cozen'd and beguil'd'), an incredulous refusal to face the fact of his defeat, which is also her own. With Edmund the acquisition of knowledge is more complex— appropriately, since he is the most intelligent of the evil characters—but in his case also its acquisition proceeds only step by step with events. He does not reveal, any more than the others, an active power to acquire it. When he realizes that he is dying he echoes Edgar's

> The Gods are just, and of our pleasant vices
> Make instruments to plague us;
> The dark and vicious place where thee he got
> Cost him his eyes. (v, iii, 170–3)

with

> Th'hast spoken right, 'tis true.
> The wheel is come full circle; I am here.

Edgar then goes on to give his account of how he has looked after their father, Gloucester, and describes his death. Edmund tells him that

> This speech of yours hath mov'd me,
> And shall perchance do good; but speak you on;
> You look as you had something more to say. (ll. 199–201)

Here, clearly, Edmund is toying with the idea of revealing that he has ordered the deaths of Lear and Cordelia; his human feeling is aroused by hearing how Edgar has looked after their father. But Edmund is not able to learn mercy merely by word or reason. In order to bring him to act mercifully an act is necessary; and this consists in the bringing in of the bodies of Goneril and Regan.[9] This makes him realize

> Yet Edmund was belov'd:
> The one the other poison'd for my sake,
> And after slew herself. (ll. 239–41)

The actual presence of the dead bodies, by bringing home to him that he was after all 'belov'd', gives him the good will which makes him, but only when it is too late, try to perform his good deed.

> I pant for life; some good I mean to do
> Despite of mine own nature. Quickly send,
> Be brief in it, to th'castle; for my writ
> Is on the life of Lear and on Cordelia.
> Nay, send in time. (ll. 243–7)

Edmund's delay, which has caused so much puzzlement, can thus be seen as part of the theme of the acquisition of knowledge.

But in the latter part of the play the evil characters are not alone in being instructed by the impact of events. So also are the good, the difference being that the events which cause an extension of their consciousness are provided by Lear and Gloucester themselves. Here the role of Lear, and to a lesser extent of Gloucester, changes into its opposite. From being the recipients of knowledge they come eventually, by their appearance at dramatically important points, to instruct others. Thus Edgar is congratulating himself that 'The lamentable change is from the best; / The worst returns to laughter' (IV, i, 5–6) when he sees the blinded Gloucester, and learns that 'the worst is not / So long as we can say "This is the worst"' (ll. 27–8). Edgar's later comment on witnessing the scene between Gloucester and Lear—'I would not take this from report; it is, / And my heart breaks at it' (IV, vi, 142–3)—explicitly affirms that the knowledge which it conveys is only to be acquired from direct experience.

The final appearance of Lear represents a further development of this change of roles. Earlier in the play his appeals to the heavens have, as a part of his tragic initiation, met with 'the sternest of replies'.[10] At the end Albany, on hearing of the danger to Cordelia, exclaims 'The gods defend her!', and his prayer is at once answered by the entry of 'Lear, *with* Cordelia *dead in his arms*'. Lear from being the instructed has become the instructor, causing Kent to liken the scene to the Last Judgment (l. 263). Far from trying to delude himself, Lear emphasizes the fact that Cordelia is dead:

> She's gone for ever.
> I know when one is dead, and when one lives;
> She's dead as earth. (ll. 259–61)

He tries, however, to find out, by objective evidence, whether there is a chance that she is still alive ('Lend me a looking-glass'), and seeing the movement of a feather thinks for a moment that she may have survived, but soon perceives that she is indeed 'gone for ever' (l. 270). He once more wonders momentarily if she lives—'Ha! / What is't thou say'st?'—but he receives no answer. His last appearance in the role of instructor occurs when Albany declares that a just settlement is to be established:

> All friends shall taste
> The wages of their virtue, and all foes
> The cup of their deservings. (ll. 302–4)

An ending of this kind may be adequate for, say, *Macbeth* (the ending of which it indeed resembles), but for this play it will not do. It is Lear himself who in his last speech and death demonstrates its inadequacy, so that Albany comes to realize that 'Our present business / Is general woe' (ll. 318–19):

> And my poor fool is hang'd! No, no, no life!
> Why should a dog, a horse, a rat, have life,
> And thou no breath at all? Thou'lt come no more,
> Never, never, never, never, never!
> Pray you, undo this button: thank you, Sir.
> Do you see this? Look on her, look, her lips,
> Look there, look there! (ll. 305–11)

If we take it that Lear finally believes that Cordelia is alive, we alter the direction of the whole movement which has been taking place throughout the play, a movement by which he attains to an ever greater consciousness and eventually becomes the agent who brings about an enlargement of the consciousness of others; and we are also guilty of confusing together Lear and the evil characters, for it is especially they who remain incapable of adequately assessing events. There is, in fact, nothing in his speech from the five-times repeated 'Never' to his last words 'look there!', which indicates a transition from grief to joy. Bradley thought that there was a cry 'represented in the oldest text by a four-times repeated "O"',[11] but since it occurs only in the Quarto it is presumably an actor's interpolation,[12] a fact of which Bradley in the then existing state of textual studies could not be expected to be aware. Cordelia's lips might, by a change in colour, give a sign of death but hardly one of life; and it is appropriate that Lear's attention should be finally concentrated on her organ of speech. As at the beginning of the play she says nothing, but this time Lear dies with the effort of realizing to the full the implications of her silence. That, and not merely despair, brings about his death. The extent of his consciousness, as well as of his sufferings, is emphasized in the concluding speech:[13]

> The oldest hath borne most: we that are young
> Shall never see so much, nor live so long.

We should remember that Bradley's interpretation of Lear's last speech finds its logical development in the view proposed by William Empson, who regards Lear in the last scene as mad again, and as, finally, the eternal fool and scapegoat who has experienced everything and learned nothing.[14] This is an interpretation which makes it difficult to regard *King Lear* as a tragedy at all. Moreover, it is only by bearing in mind the active role of Lear's progress towards knowledge that we can see the later part of the play as having a convincing dramatic form. D. G. James, who interprets the whole drama as a process of discovery not so much by Lear as by Shakespeare himself, follows Granville-Barker in thinking that in the last two acts the best things 'will be incidental and not germane to the actual story'.[15] If we see the

73

active and central role as residing elsewhere than in Lear, the last two acts are indeed dramatically unconvincing, with the main emphasis on Edgar as a fighting man and Cordelia as the leader of an army. James remarks that 'the souls of Cordelia and Edgar are not in the stage figures who in battle and combat thus serve the purposes of a plot which a dramatist has to get on with and bring to a conclusion'.[16] But Cordelia and Edgar appear unreal only if we see the active roles they are given as occupying the centre of the dramatic movement. With the main interest concentrated on the development of Lear, the presentation of Edgar as a fighting man and Cordelia as the leader of an army does not have to be any less perfunctory than it actually is; and 'the soul of the play and the body of the plot' do not, as James suggests,[17] fall apart.

NOTES

1. In *Shakespearean Tragedy* (1904; ed. 1905), p. 291.

2. It has, for example, been accepted by H. Granville-Barker, *Prefaces to Shakespeare: First Series* (1927), p. 185, n. 1; R. W. Chambers, 'King Lear', *W. P. Ker Memorial Lecture* (1939; Glasgow, 1940), pp. 44 ff.; William Empson, *The Structure of Complex Words* (1951), pp. 151 ff.; Kenneth Muir, The New Arden ed. (1952), p. lix.

3. In three recent extensive studies of *King Lear*—see R. B. Heilman, *This Great Stage* (Louisiana State University Press, 1948); J. F. Danby, *Shakespeare's Doctrine of Nature* (1949); D. G. James, *The Dream of Learning* (Oxford, 1951) —the suggestion is not discussed at all. Heilman (p. 54) remarks non-committally that Lear 'strains frantically, possibly convinced that he does see life'. Danby merely observes (p. 195) that Lear in the last scene is 'mad again'. James does not refer to Bradley's suggestion.

4. Already, just before going out into the storm, Lear replies to Regan's 'What need one?' with

> O! reason not the need; our basest beggars
> Are in the poorest thing superfluous: (II, iv, 266–7)

but while this may to some extent announce his later capacity for generalizing his experiences, here the generalization is merely part of the argument with which he attacks Regan.

5. Quotations are from *King Lear*, ed. K. Muir.

6. One indication of Gloucester's lesser stature is that he has to be helped in his acquisition of knowledge by Edgar, whereas Lear learns essentially through his own efforts. The comments of the Fool, though illuminating, only emphasize those things which Lear already suspects. These comments in no way represent an equivalent to Edgar's guidance of Gloucester.

7. *Shakespearean Tragedy*, p. 290.

8. See Muir, ed. cit. p. 201. In a sense Lear's words in II, iv, 286–8 ('this heart / Shall break into a hundred thousand flaws / Or ere I'll weep') are also true—he does go mad rather than weep and capitulate—but in the context these words are associated with his empty threats of revenge.

9. It is true that Albany has already (l. 237) asked Edmund where Lear and Cordelia are, but the dying Edmund need not have answered, and it is only after the speeches in ll. 239–42 that he gives the necessary information. Moreover, it is clear from the speech, quoted below, in which he tells of their danger that he is now genuinely anxious that the reprieve should reach them in time.

10. The phrase used by Bradley, *Shakespearean Tragedy*, p. 274.

11. *Ibid.* p. 291.

12. See *King Lear*, ed. G. I. Duthie (Oxford, 1949), p. 44. The four-times repeated 'O' occurs after 'thank you, Sir' (l. 309). Far from representing a transition to Lear's last words the 'O's are meant to be his dying groans; they, in fact, take the place of his last words (ll. 310–11) which are found only in the Folio. It is these last words in ll. 310–11 which Bradley thinks express the ecstasy of joy from which Lear dies. If the Quarto version gives anything approximating to the stage presentation of his death, he clearly cannot have been presented as dying from joy rather than grief.

13. In the Folio the last speech is given, correctly, to Edgar; in the Quarto it is given to Albany.

14. See *The Structure of Complex Words*, pp. 151 ff. Empson, referring to Lear's 'And my poor fool is hang'd!', suggests (p. 152) that 'Lear is now thrown back into something like the storm phase of his madness, the effect of immediate shock, and the Fool seems to him part of it'. But 'fool' was a term of endearment (see *O.E.D.* 'Fool', sb.¹, 1*c*), and even if we think that there is an association in Lear's mind between the Fool and Cordelia, the connection is natural, for the Fool like Cordelia has the merit of speaking the truth. Lear's earlier remoteness, after his entry with Cordelia dead in his arms, from what is taking place around him is the result of his new-found union with her. His sense of this union has been given expression in his 'Come, let's away to prison' speech, and makes all the greater his concentration on the fact of her death.

15. See *The Dream of Learning*, p. 112.

16. *Ibid.* p. 113.

17. *Ibid.* p. 112. Bradley himself, since he sees Lear as essentially passive, is driven to the unsatisfactory conclusion that 'it is impossible...from the point of view of construction, to regard the hero as the leading figure' (*op. cit.* p. 53). From the viewpoint of construction he thus regards Goneril, Regan and Edmund as the leading characters. This suggests that there is in *King Lear* a serious discrepancy between form and content.

THE CATHARSIS OF *KING LEAR*

BY

J. STAMPFER

The overriding critical problem in *King Lear* is that of its ending. The deaths of Lear and Cordelia confront us like a raw, fresh wound where our every instinct calls for healing and reconciliation. This problem, moreover, is as much one of philosophic order as of dramatic effect. In what sort of universe, we ask ourselves, can wasteful death follow suffering and torture? Nor is this concern an extrapolation from our own culture. It is, rather, implicit in Lear's own image, when he calls for tongues and eyes to howl 'That heaven's vault should crack' (v, iii, 259), and in his despairing question:

> Why should a dog, a horse, a rat, have life,
> And thou no breath at all? (v, iii, 306–7)

The problem becomes more overwhelming when we consider that, unlike the problems Shakespeare may have inherited with the plot of *Hamlet*, this tragic ending was imposed by Shakespeare on a story which, in its source, allowed Cordelia's forces to win the war. Moreover, the massive intrusion into *King Lear* of Christian elements of providence, depravity, and spiritual regeneration make it impossible to shunt aside the ending as a coincidence of its pre-Christian setting. The antiquity of setting may have had the irrelevant effect of releasing certain inhibitions in the playwright's mind; but the playgoers in Shakespeare's audience did not put on pagan minds to see the play. Rather, the constant references to retributive justice, perhaps greater here than in any other of Shakespeare's tragedies, make it an issue in a way that it is not in such 'pagan' plays as *Timon of Athens*, *Antony and Cleopatra*, and *Coriolanus*. Indeed, part of the poignance of *King Lear* lies in the fact that its issues, and the varieties of evil that it faces, are so central to Christianity, while it is denied any of the mitigation offered by a well-defined heaven and hell, and a formal doctrine of supernatural salvation.

The impression of unreconciled savagery and violence in the ending has been mitigated, in our generation, by a critical reading that would interpret Lear's last emotion as one of joy, even ecstasy, rather than one of unbearable agony. Bradley advances this reading, though hedged with a considerable qualification, in the following passage:

And, finally, though he is killed by an agony of pain, the agony in which he actually dies is not one of pain but of ecstasy. Suddenly, with a cry represented in the oldest text by a four-times repeated 'O', he exclaims:

> Do you see this? Look on her, look, her lips,
> Look there, look there!

These are the last words of Lear. He is sure, at last, that she *lives*: and what had he said when he was still in doubt?

> She lives! if it be so,
> It is a chance which doth redeem all sorrows
> That ever I have felt!

77

To us, perhaps, the knowledge that he is deceived may bring a culmination of pain: but, if it brings *only* that, I believe we are false to Shakespeare, and it seems almost beyond question that any actor is false to the text who does not attempt to express, in Lear's last accents and gestures and look, an unbearable *joy*.[1]

Some recent critics[2] have gone much further than Bradley in an attempt to build from Lear's momentary emotion at death a 'chance which doth redeem all sorrows', and make the play's ending a transfigured vision of attained salvation.

Before disputing the weight this penultimate moment in Lear's life can bear in counterbalancing all that precedes it, one must first consider whether the reading itself is defensible; for, in a sense, everything in the play hangs in the balance with Lear's death. If it is one of transfiguring joy, then one might, for all the enormous difficulties involved, affirm that a species of order is re-established. If not, however, then the impression is irresistible that in *King Lear* Shakespeare was confronting chaos itself, unmitigated, brutal, and utterly unresolved. The problems of justice and order, however interpreted, finally rest in the mystery of Lear's last moment, and not in the ambiguity of whether Edgar will or will not take over, by default, the throne of England. Like the news of Edmund's death, the problem of the succession is 'but a trifle' (v, iii, 295) alongside the supreme issue of whether any 'comfort' was applied by Shakespeare to the 'great decay' of Lear, as was evidently applied by him to the deaths of Hamlet and to a lesser extent Othello.

Bradley and those who follow him in this matter rest their case on the observation that Lear died persuaded that Cordelia still lived. He leaves unremarked, however, the fact that this illusion is not a new and sudden turn, but recurs three or four times in the last scene. It is, indeed, the main concern of Lear's first three speeches on re-entering the stage, before he goes temporarily out of his mind:

She's gone for ever!

I know when one is dead, and when one lives;
She's dead as earth. Lend me a looking glass;
If that her breath will mist or stain the stone,
Why, then she lives.

(v, iii, 259–63)

The tension here, and it is the underlying tension in Lear until his death, lies between an absolute knowledge that Cordelia is dead, and an absolute inability to accept it. Lear 'knows when one is dead, and when one lives'. His very faculties of reason and knowledge would be in question if he could not distinguish life from death. 'She's gone for ever...She's dead as earth', he repeats over and over. If he is to grasp reality in the face of madness, it is the reality of Cordelia's death that he must grasp. But this is the one reality that sears him whenever he attempts to grasp it, and so he tries, by the test of the looking glass, to prove that she lives, despite his emphatically underlined knowledge to the contrary.

Three brief speeches by Kent, Edgar and Albany intervene between this and Lear's next speech. One would guess that Lear is very active on stage at this point, possibly getting a looking glass, holding it up to Cordelia's lips, registering either momentary hope or immediate despair, then, when this test fails, snatching a feather and trying a second test. He would seem to be oblivious to all reality but Cordelia's body and his attempts to prove that she is alive. His second speech shows what is at stake in the effort:

> This feather stirs; she lives! If it be so,
> It is a chance which does redeem all sorrows
> That ever I have felt.   (ll. 265–7)

This effort, too, fails, and Kent's painful attempt, on his knees, to wrest Lear's attention away from Cordelia only makes Lear momentarily turn on his companions with the savage outcry of 'murderers' and 'traitors' before trying again to prove her alive, this time by putting his ear to her lips in the thought that she might be speaking:

> A plague upon you, murderers, traitors all:
> I might have sav'd her; now she's gone for ever!
> Cordelia! Cordelia! stay a little. Ha!
> What is't thou say'st? Her voice was ever soft,
> Gentle, and low; an excellent thing in woman.
> I kill'd the slave that was a-hanging thee.   (ll. 269–74)

His outcry, 'Ha!', like his cry 'This feather stirs', registers an illusion that Cordelia has spoken to him. This is a wilder self-deception than the thought that she has breathed, and remains with him beyond the end of the speech. His 'I kill'd the slave' is said almost lovingly and protectively to Cordelia's body, as if she heard him. Thus he struggles simultaneously for sanity and for the belief that Cordelia lives. Under the strain of these two irreconcilable psychic needs, his mind simply slips and relaxes into temporary madness:

> He knows not what he says; and vain is it
> That we present us to him.   (ll. 293–4)

But agonized sanity breaks through Lear's madness once more, as the words of Kent, Albany and Edgar could not. Albany sees it rising, ominously convulsing Lear's features, and exclaims, 'O, see, see!' (l. 304) as Lear cries out:

> And my poor fool is hang'd! No, no, no life!
> Why should a dog, a horse, a rat, have life,
> And thou no breath at all? Thou'lt come no more,
> Never, never, never, never, never!   (ll. 305–8)

The repeated cries of 'Never!' are the steady hammering of truth on a mind unable to endure it. Lear's life-blood rushes to his head. He chokes, and asks someone to undo the button of his collar (l. 309). Then, against the unendurable pressure of reality, the counterbalancing illusion that Cordelia lives rushes forth once more. Once again, it is at her lips, breathing or speaking, that he seeks life and dies:

> Do you see this? Look on her, look, her lips,
> Look there, look there! (*dies*)   (ll. 310–11)

Who is to say, given this cycle of despair, insanity, and the illusion of hope, if it really matters at what point of the cycle Lear expires, or even if his last words establish it decisively? On the contrary, on purely aesthetic grounds, we have an indication from another point in Act v that all of Lear's emotions have been gathering to an unendurable head at the moment of death. Gloucester, the counterpart to Lear in the subplot, was, like him, driven out by his false offspring, tormented in the storm, and finally preserved by a faithful, though rejected child. And Gloucester's death, which is described in considerable detail by Edgar, contains just such a welter of conflicting feelings as does Lear's, and might well be the model for understanding Lear's death:

> Never,—O fault!—reveal'd myself unto him,
> Until some half-hour past, when I was arm'd.
> Not sure, though hoping, of this good success,
> I ask'd his blessing, and from first to last
> Told him our pilgrimage; but his flaw'd heart,
> Alack, too weak the conflict to support!
> 'Twixt two extremes of passion, joy and grief,
> Burst smilingly.   (v, iii, 192–9)

Gloucester's heart burst from its inability to contain two conflicting emotions, his psyche torn apart by a thunderclap of simultaneous joy and grief. And such, by aesthetic parallel, we may presume was the death of Lear, whose 'flaw'd heart', too, as is evident throughout the last scene, was

> Alack, too weak the conflict to support!

But the similarity only serves to accentuate the basic difference between the two deaths. Gloucester died between extremes of joy and grief, at the knowledge that his son was miraculously preserved, Lear between extremes of illusion and truth, ecstasy and the blackest despair, at the knowledge that his daughter was needlessly butchered. Gloucester's heart 'burst smilingly' at his reunion with Edgar; Lear's, we are driven to conclude, burst in the purest agony at his eternal separation from Cordelia.

There is, then, no mitigation in Lear's death, hence no mitigation in the ending of the play. On the contrary, either the play has no aesthetic unity, or everything in it, including Lear's spiritual regeneration, is instrumental to the explosive poignance of Lear's death. Nor can there be any blenching from the implications of Lear's last sane question:

> Why should a dog, a horse, a rat, have life,
> And thou no breath at all? Thou'lt come no more.
> Never, never, never, never, never!

It is only by giving Lear's death a fleeting, ecstatic joy that Bradley can read some sort of reconciliation into the ending, some renewed synthesis of cosmic goodness to follow an antithesis of pure evil. Without it, this is simply, as Lear recognized, a universe where dogs, horses, and rats live, and Cordelias are butchered. There may be mitigations in man himself, but none in the world which surrounds him. Indeed, unless Lear's death is a thoroughly anomalous postscript to his pilgrimage of life, the most organic view of the plot would make almost a test case of Lear, depicting, through his life and death, a universe in which even those who have fully repented, done penance, and risen to the tender regard of sainthood[3] can be hunted down, driven insane, and killed by the most agonizing extremes of passion.

The plot of *King Lear* is generally not read in this fashion. On the contrary, its denouement is generally interpreted as another 'turn of the screw', an added, and unnecessary, twist of horror to round out a play already sated with horrors. If it is defended, it is generally on grounds like those of Lamb,[4] who contended that it was a 'fair dismissal' from life after all Lear had suffered, or those of Bradley, that Lear's death is a transfiguration of joy to counterbalance all that has preceded it. Neither reading is satisfactory, Lamb's because it makes the ending, at best, an epilogue rather than a denouement to the main body of the action, Bradley's because the textual evidence points to the opposite interpretation of Lear's death. If Lear's spiritual regeneration, however, with the fearful penance he endures, is taken as the play's 'middle', and his death, despite that regeneration, as its denouement, then the catharsis of *King Lear*, Shakespeare's profoundest tragedy, has as yet escaped definition. This catharsis, grounded in the most universal elements of the human condition, can be formulated only when one has drawn together some of the relevant philosophical issues of the play.

Thus, the ending is decisive in resolving the plethora of attitudes presented in the play concerning the relationship between God and man. Set side by side, out of context, and unrelated to the denouement, these attitudes, and their religious frames of reference, can be made to appear an absolute chaos. Certainly almost every possible point of view on the gods and cosmic justice is expressed, from a malevolent, wanton polytheism (IV, i, 38–9) to an astrological determinism (IV, iii, 34–5), from an amoral, personified Nature-goddess (I, ii, 1) to 'high-judging Jove' (II, iv, 231). But the very multitude, concern, and contradictory character of these references do not cancel each other out, but rather show how precarious is the concept of cosmic justice. Surely if the play's ending is an ending, and cosmic justice has hung in the balance with such matters as Goneril's cruelty (IV, ii, 46–50), Gloucester's blinding (III, vii, 99–100), and Edmund's death (V, iii, 174), it collapses with Lear's ultimate question: 'Why should a dog, a horse, a rat, have life, / And thou no breath at all?' Despite the pagan setting, the problem of theodicy, the justification of God's way with man, is invoked by so many characters, and with such concern, that it emerges as a key issue in the play. As such, either the denouement vindicates it, or its integrity is universally destroyed. In point of fact, this is implied in the deaths of Lear and Cordelia.

The force of evil, perhaps the most dynamic element in the Christian tragedies, is extended to wide dimensions in *King Lear*, where two distinct modes of evil emerge, evil as animalism, in Goneril and Regan, and evil as doctrinaire atheism, in Edmund. These modes are not to be confused. Goneril, in particular, is, from the point of view of conscience, an animal or beast of prey. She and Regan never discuss doctrine, as does Edmund, or offer motives, as does Iago. Their actions have the immediacy of animals, to whom consideration never interposes between appetite and deed. It is in this spirit that Lear compares Goneril, in a single scene (I, iv), to a sea-monster, a detested kite, a serpent and a wolf, and Albany, in another (IV, ii), to a tiger, a bear, a monster of the deep, and a fiend, as though, through them, animalism were bursting through civil society.

Edmund, on the other hand, is a doctrinaire atheist, with regard not only to God, but also to the traditional, organic universe, a heterodoxy equally horrifying to the Elizabethans. This doctrinaire atheism involves an issue as basic in *King Lear* as that of a retributive justice, and that is the bond between man, society and nature. Here, there is no plethora of attitudes, but two positions, essentially, that of Cordelia, and that of Edmund. Cordelia's position is perhaps best expressed by Albany, after he learns of Goneril's treatment of Lear:

> That nature which contemns its origin
> Cannot be bordered certain in itself.
> She that herself will sliver and disbranch
> From her material sap, perforce must wither
> And come to desperate use. (IV, ii, 32–6)

According to Albany, an invisible bond of sympathy binds human beings like twigs to the branches of a tree. This bond is no vague universal principle, but closely rooted in one's immediate family and society. This is natural law in its most elemental possible sense, not a moral code, but almost a biochemical reaction. Hierarchical propriety is a necessity for life, like sunlight and water, its violation an act of suicide or perversion. It is Cordelia, in response to this law, who says firmly, 'I love your majesty / According to my bond; no more nor less' (I, i, 94–5). This bond, the central concept of the play, is the bond of nature, made up at once of propriety and charity.

In contrast to this concept of Nature is Edmund's soliloquy affirming his doctrinaire atheism (I, ii, 1–15), where natural law is summed up in two phrases, 'the plague of custom', and 'the curiosity of nations'. The bond of human relations, as understood by Cordelia and Albany, is a tissue of extraneous, artificial constraints. Edmund recognizes a hierarchy, but rather than growing out of society, this hierarchy goes wholly against its grain. This is the hierarchy of animal vitality, by which 'the lusty stealth of nature', even in the act of adultery, creates a more worthy issue than the 'dull, stale, tired bed' of marriage. And in response to Gloucester's superstitious references to the larger concept of the organic universe, Edmund repudiates any relationship between the 'orbs from whom we do exist' and his own destiny (I, ii, 139–45).

Strangely enough, however, while the denouement seems to destroy any basis for providential justice, it would seem to vindicate Cordelia with regard to the bond of human nature. Thus, the deaths of Cornwall, Goneril, and Regan are, as Albany prophesied, the swift and monstrous preying of humanity upon itself. Cornwall is killed by his own servant; Regan is poisoned by her sister; and Goneril finally commits suicide. Even more is Cordelia vindicated in Edmund, who is mortally wounded by his brother, and then goes through a complete, and to this reader, sincere repentance before his death. Critics have expressed bewilderment at Edmund's delay in attempting to save Lear and Cordelia. They do not, however, remark the significance of the point at which Edmund acts. For it is not until Goneril confesses the poisoning of Regan and commits suicide, thus persuading Edmund that he was loved, that he bestirs himself to save Lear and Cordelia if it is not too late. Intellectual assent is not sufficient. Only to those wholly caught up in the bond of love is charity possible:

> *Edm.* Yet Edmund was belov'd:
> The one the other poison'd for my sake,
> And after slew herself.
> *Alb.* Even so. Cover their faces.
> *Edm.* I pant for life. Some good I mean to do,
> Despite of mine own nature. (V, iii, 239–44)

Herein, however, lies a sardonic paradox; for Edmund deceived himself. He was the object of lust, but was not encompassed by love. Goneril slew Regan for his sake, but it was out of lust and ambition; she was incapable of that love which brings to self-transcendence, such as Cordelia's love of Lear, or his own act of 'good', in spite of his 'own nature'. And far from killing herself for Edmund's sake, she committed suicide, utterly alone, at the implicit threat of arrest for treason. Edmund, ever the doctrinaire logician, took false evidence of the bond of love at face value, and died as isolated as he lived. The two forms of evil in *King Lear* were ultimately opaque to one another.

But an even more sardonic paradox is implicit in Edmund's death. For Edmund, by abandoning his atheistic faith and acknowledging the power of love, accepts Cordelia's instinctual affirmation of natural law. But the denouement itself, with the gratuitous, harrowing deaths of Cordelia and Lear, controverts any justice in the universe. Chance kills, in despite of the maidenly stars. It would seem, then, by the denouement, that the universe belongs to Edmund, but mankind belongs to Cordelia. In a palsied cosmos, orphan man must either live by the moral law, which is the bond of love, or swiftly destroy himself. To this paradox, too, Shakespeare offers no mitigation in *King Lear*. The human condition is as inescapable as it is unendurable.

To so paradoxical an ending, what catharsis is possible? This question can be answered only by re-examining the structure of the plot. There can be observed, in *Hamlet*, a radical break from the mode of redemption in such earlier plays as *Romeo and Juliet*. In *Romeo and Juliet*, redemption comes when the tragic hero affirms the traditional frame of values of society, love, an appropriate marriage, peace, and the like, though society has, in practice, ceased to follow them. The result is to enhance the *sancta* of society by the sacrifice of life itself. In *Hamlet*, redemption only comes, finally, when the tragic hero spurns and transcends the *sancta* of society, and appeals to a religious mysticism into which human wisdom can have no entry, and in which, at most, 'the readiness is all'. The final result, however, is none the less the redemption of society and the reconciliation of the tragic hero to it; for Hamlet's last act is to cast a decisive vote for the next king of Denmark. Even *Othello*, domestic tragedy though it is, ends with the reconciliation of the tragic hero and society; and Othello's last act is an affirmation of loyalty to Venice and the execution of judgement upon himself. *King Lear* is Shakespeare's first tragedy in which the tragic hero dies unreconciled and indifferent to society.

The opening movement of *King Lear* is, then, not merely a physical exile from, but an abandonment of the formal *sancta* and institutions of society, which is pictured as even more bankrupt than in *Hamlet*. In *Hamlet*, only one man's deliberate crime corrupts the Danish state, 'mining all within'; in *King Lear*, animalism, atheism, brutal ambition, superstition, self-indulgence, and lethargy all contribute to society's decay. In this opening movement of abandonment, Lear is stripped of all that majesty and reverence clothing him in the opening scene, of kingdom, family, retainers, shelter, and finally reason and clothing themselves, until he comes, at the nadir of his fortunes, to 'the thing itself...a poor bare forked animal' (III, iv, 111–12). Romeo found his touchstone of truth against the rich texture of the Capulet feast, Lear in an abandoned and naked madman. Romeo and Juliet formed, from the first, an inviolate circle of innocence that was the fulfilment of their previous lives; Lear found no innocence until all his previous life had been stripped away from him.

In contrast to this movement of abandonment, and the basis of the second, counter-movement, stands not, as in *Hamlet*, religious mysticism, but an elemental bond that we can, in this play, indifferently call charity or natural law, one that binds man to man, child to parent, husband to wife, and servant to master almost by a biological impulsion. From first to last, charity is discovered, not as the crown of power and earthly blessing, but in their despite. This theme is enunciated by France in taking Cordelia for his wife:

> Fairest Cordelia, that art most rich being poor,
> Most choice forsaken, and most lov'd despis'd!
> Thee and thy virtues here I seize upon,
> Be it lawful I take up what's cast away.
> Gods, gods! 'tis strange that from their cold'st neglect
> My love should kindle to inflam'd respect. (I, i, 253–8)

The same affirmation is made by Kent, in entering the impoverished Lear's service:

> *Lear.* If thou be'st as poor for a subject as he's for a king, thou art poor
> enough. What wouldst thou?
> *Kent.* Service.
> *Lear.* Who wouldst thou serve?
> *Kent.* You.
> *Lear.* Dost thou know me, fellow?
> *Kent.* No, sir; but you have that in your countenance which I would fain
> call master.
> *Lear.* What's that?
> *Kent.* Authority. (I, iv, 22–32)

Indeed, organized society dulls people to an awareness of charity, so that it is only in Lear's abandonment that he becomes bound to all men:

> Poor naked wretches, wheresoe'er you are,
> That bide the pelting of this pitiless storm,
> How shall your houseless heads and unfed sides,
> Your loop'd and window'd raggedness, defend you
> From seasons such as these? O, I have ta'en
> Too little care of this! Take physic, pomp;
> Expose thyself to what these wretches feel,
> That thou may'st shake the superflux to them,
> And show the heavens more just. (III, iv, 28–36)

Shakespeare could, of course, have used this more elemental level of charity or natural law as he used the force of love in *Romeo and Juliet*, to redeem and renew society. Had he chosen to do so, it would have become politically effective in Cordelia's invading army, overwhelmed the corrupt elements then in power, and restored the throne to Lear, as is suggested in Shakespeare's conventionally pious source. But society, in Shakespeare, is now no longer capable of self-renewal. And so the counter-movement of the play, the reclothing of Lear, by charity and natural law, with majesty, sanity, family and shelter, after the most terrible of penances, does not close the play. At its close, the completion only of its dramatic 'middle', Lear is utterly purged of soul, while the hierarchy of society is reduced, as at the end of *Hamlet*, to an equation of 'court news' with 'gilded butterflies' (v, iii, 13–14). At this point, if the universe of the play contained a transcendent providence, it should act as in the closing movement of *Hamlet*, mysteriously to redeem a society unable to redeem itself.

Shakespeare's pessimism, however, has deepened since *Hamlet*, and the deaths to no purpose of Lear and Cordelia controvert any providential redemption in the play's decisive, closing movement, so that another resolution entirely is called for. Narrowing our problem somewhat, the catharsis of any play lies in the relationship of the denouement to the expectations set up in the play's 'middle'. In *King Lear*, this middle movement has to do primarily with Lear's spiritual regeneration after his 'stripping' in the opening movement of the play. These two movements can be subsumed in a single great cycle, from hauteur and spiritual blindness through purgative suffering to humility and spiritual vision, a cycle that reaches its culmination in Lear's address of consolation to Cordelia before they are taken off to prison (v, iii, 9–17). The catharsis of *King Lear* would seem to lie, then, in the challenge of Lear's subsequent death to the penance and spiritual transcendence that culminates the play's second movement. This challenge can be described as follows:—

All men, in all societies, make, as it were, a covenant with society in their earliest infancy. By this covenant, the dawning human consciousness accepts society's deepest ordinances, beliefs, and moral standards in exchange for a promise of whatever rewards and blessings society offers. The notion of intelligible reward and punishment, whether formulated as a theological doctrine and called retributive justice or as a psychological doctrine and called the reality principle, is as basic to human nature as the passions themselves. But given the contingency of human life, that covenant is constantly broken by corruption within and without. A man's life and that of his family are at all times hostages of his limited wisdom, his tainted morality, the wayward-ness of chance, and the decay of institutions. Indeed, social ritual, whether religious in character, like confession or periodic fasting, or secular, like the ceremonial convening of a legislature, is an attempt to strengthen the bond of a covenant inevitably weakened by the attrition of evil and the brute passage of time. These are all, in a sense, acts of penance, that is, acts whose deepest intent is to purge us of guilt and the fear of being abandoned, to refresh our bond with one another and with our private and collective destiny.

Lear, at the beginning of the play, embodies all that man looks forward to in a world in which, ultimately, nothing is secure. He has vocation, age, wealth, monarchy, family, personal fol-lowers and long experience. Like Oedipus and Othello, he would have seemed to have attained, before the play begins, what men strive for with indifferent success all their lives. In this sense, Lear engages our sympathies as an archetype of mankind. And just as Othello discovers areas of experience which he never cultivated and which destroy him, Lear discovers that even in those areas he most cultivated he has nothing. Thus, like Oedipus and more than Othello, Lear activates the latent anxiety at the core of the human condition, the fear not only of unexpected catastrophe but that even what seems like success may be a delusion, masking corruption, crime and almost consummated failure.

This opening movement, however, leads not to dissolution, exposure and self-recognition, as in *Oedipus* and *Othello*, but to purgation. And Lear's purgation, by the end of the play's middle movement, like his gifts and his vulnerability at its start, is so complete as to be archetypal. By the time he enters prison, he has paid every price and been stripped of everything a man can lose, even his sanity, in payment for folly and pride. He stands beyond the veil of fire, momentarily serene and alive. As such he activates an even profounder fear than the fear of failure, and that is the fear that whatever penance a man may pay may not be enough once the machinery of destruction has been let loose, because the partner of his covenant may be neither grace nor the balance of law, but malignity, intransigence or chaos.

The final, penultimate tragedy of Lear, then, is not the tragedy of *hubris*, but the tragedy of penance. When Lear, the archetype not of a proud, but of a penitential man, brutally dies, then the uttermost that can happen to man has happened. One can rationalize a passing pedestrian struck down by a random automobile; there is no blenching from this death. Each audience harbours this anxiety in moments of guilt and in acts of penance. And with Lear's death, each audience, by the ritual of the drama, shares and releases the most private and constricting fear to which mankind is subject, the fear that penance is impossible, that the covenant, once broken, can never be re-established, because its partner has no charity, resilience, or harmony—the fear, in other words, that we inhabit an imbecile universe. It is by this vision of reality that Lear lays down his life for his folly. Within its bounds lies the catharsis of Shakespeare's profoundest tragedy.

NOTES

1. A. C. Bradley, *Shakespearean Tragedy* (1924), p. 291.

2. Harold S. Wilson, *On the Design of Shakespearean Tragedy* (Toronto, 1957), p. 204; Geoffrey Bush, *Shakespeare and the Natural Condition* (Cambridge, Mass., 1956), p. 128.

3. L. L. Schücking, in his *Character Problems in Shakespeare's Plays* (New York, 1922), p. 186, cites most, though not all the evidence that can be offered to document a spiritual regeneration in Lear, only to deny it any validity in the play because, by the comparative method, he finds no similar concern elsewhere in Shakespeare for *charitas*, or social justice. Aside from a number of relevant passages that leap to mind from other plays, the most striking parallel is in *King Lear*, itself, where Gloucester, Lear's counterpart in the subplot, makes a speech similar to Lear's prayer, though not as profound, on the poor and the wretched (IV, i, 67–74). Whatever may or may not be true in other plays, charity is apparently a prime consideration in *King Lear*; and, if so, Lear's regeneration in charity is, by Schücking's own evidence, part of the play's aesthetic movement.

4. New Variorum edition of *King Lear* (Philadelphia, 1880), p. 421.

COSTUME IN *KING LEAR*

BY

W. MOELWYN MERCHANT

The greater number of the illustrations to *King Lear*, whether in frontispieces and other published engravings or in easel pictures, are set on the heath during the storm. Rarely in Shakespeare has costume played so full a part either in direct stage business or in symbolic action as in these scenes on the heath. The argument sways uncertainly in Lear's mind through a complete circle to revulsion; in compassionate prudence he counsels Edgar:

Why, thou wert better in thy grave, than to answer with thy uncovered body, this extremity of the skies. (III, iv, 105–6)

and this momentary insight into dereliction, in its pity for Edgar's nakedness, is pointed by the contrast with the 'courtly' costumes of the Fool, Kent and Lear himself, who are all indebted to the worm and the beast for their 'lendings'. Edgar's previous speech to Lear had approved in advance his rejection of a garment's 'sophistication', and with precisely Lear's choice of hide and silk:

Let not the creaking of shoes nor the rustling of silks, betray thy poor heart to woman. (III, iv, 97–9)

Edgar and Lear take up the same theme in the fourth act. Edgar obliquely declares his constancy to his father in the ambiguous words:

> You're much deceived: in nothing am I changed
> But in my garments (IV, vi, 9–10)

and in the same scene (IV, vi) Lear returns to his former argument:

> Through tatter'd clothes small vices do appear;
> Robes and furr'd gowns hide all. Plate sin with gold,
> And the strong lance of justice hurtless breaks;
> Arm it in rags, a pigmy's straw does pierce it. (IV, vi, 168–71)

Yet vesture has its positive significance; at the reunion of Cordelia with Kent and then with her father, her first request to Kent is that he Be better suited,
> These weeds are memories of those worser hours:
> I prithee, put them off. (IV, vii, 6–8)

Her immediate concern for her father's condition, 'Is he array'd?', is answered by the Gentleman's assurance: in the heaviness of his sleep
> We put fresh garments on him (IV, vii, 21–2)

and Lear himself, in his continued mental chaos, directs attention to these new regal garments, to which he is not yet suited: all the skill I have
> Remembers not these garments. (IV, vii, 66–7)

87

To the end of the tragedy Lear is not to resume the 'Rule' of which he had shown such anxiety to 'divest' himself.

If any coherent conclusions are to be drawn from the multitude of paintings and engravings which attempt to realize in theatrical costume this aspect of the interior tragedy, there must be sharp selection. With few exceptions, it is profitable to consider mainly the costumes of Lear, Cordelia, Edgar and the Fool. There are one or two drawings of Lear in full regal costume and this survives in varying degrees into the storm scenes; Cordelia will be found throughout the eighteenth century in tolerably modish costume until Regency fashions introduced a new 'Classical' approach. No trace of the sixteenth- and seventeenth-century engravings of Bedlam Beggars appears to survive in the presentation of Edgar; as we shall find, the early illustrated Shakespeares in the eighteenth century establish his costume in strict conformity with the descriptions in the text. The Fool is the most complex figure. In the course of the eighteenth century we shall find many different survivals: the 'motley' described by Leslie Hotson;[1] the young and helpless figure which is implied in Lear's words, 'In Boy; go first, you houseless poverty'; a *commedia dell'arte* figure mediated for the eighteenth-century stage by the paintings of Watteau; and, finally, persisting through all these variants on Shakespeare's Fool, the traditional figure in coxcomb and bells, found, among Shakespeare's immediate predecessors and contemporaries, in Greene's *Friar Bacon and Friar Bungay* ('Naturall Idiots and Fooles...weare in their Cappes, cockes feathers or a hat with a necke and heade of a cocke on the top, and a bell theron') and in Whitney's *Choice of Emblemes*, where the costume is cited complete: 'A motley coate, a cockescombe, or a bell.'[2]

Three frontispieces, the engravings for Rowe's editions of 1709 and 1714, and Hayman's drawing engraved by Gravelot for Hanmer's edition of 1744, establish the manner of presentation for the first half of the eighteenth century. There is an unusually sharp distinction between 'literary' and 'theatrical' comment in the two Rowe engravings. In the frontispiece for the 1709 edition (Pl. I*a*), Kent and Gloucester urge the distracted Lear towards the thatched hovel which was to reappear in this form throughout the century; all three are in the 'modern dress' of current theatre usage. Edgar as Poor Tom is, however, unusually elaborately costumed (most subsequent engravings suggest only the Fool's comment, 'Nay, he reserved a blanket, else we had been all shamed') but there are two details, the wisps of straw bound in at the calves and the stout staff, which become established for almost all his later appearances. Du Guernier's crude engraving for the 1714 edition (Pl. I*b*) has a more elaborate group based on Shakespeare's text rather than on Nahum Tate's, from which the Fool was excluded. The gestures and attitudes ingeniously suggest fragments of speeches from a considerable part of III, iv. Lear plucks at his garments at 'Off, off you Lendings', while the Fool admonishes him, 'Prithee, nuncle, be contented, 'tis a naughty night to swim in'; the stage direction, '*Enter Gloucester, with a Torch*', is therefore anticipated, with his gesture to the hovel, 'Go in with me'. Kent is an indeterminate figure, and Edgar, bonneted as in the 1709 engraving, is distinguished by little more than his staff. There is not much to be said about the costume in this undistinguished little drawing; the Fool, Lear and Gloucester have suggestions of ruffs at the neck, perhaps an antique gesture. Hayman's frontispiece (Pl. I*c*) has the distinction that we find in all the drawings for Sir

Thomas Hanmer's edition of 1744.[3] Edgar, with blanket, staff and straw, is established as the recognizable stage figure of the next century or so; Kent is a roughly dignified figure, but Lear's costume is ambiguous. It is possible that Hayman's drawing reflects Garrick's performance at Goodman's Fields in the 1741/2 season, for, as we shall see, they were in friendly correspondence about the role at this time; certainly the drawing anticipates Garrick's Lear of twelve years later and in general the costume resembles his. But the simple strap-work decoration where Garrick was to use ermine, and the odd suggestion of smocking on the vest, tone down the regality (though Lear's hose and shoes have an elegance greater than Garrick's; cf. Pl. I*d*). The Fool again sends us back beyond Tate; he wears a rather poverty-stricken version of the garb shown in Du Guernier's engraving in 1714.

We have very full indications of Garrick's costuming for his *Lear* productions. There are many versions of Benjamin Wilson's painting (which has some of Zoffany's authority[4]) and a portion of the McArdell mezzotint is reproduced here at Pl. I*d*. A. C. Sprague comments on 'something of a novelty', that Garrick 'and the other actors in his production were "judiciously habited", not in contemporary, but in old English dresses'.[5] This is not readily apparent in the engraving, and Garrick as Lear preserves something of the tradition, found also in productions of *Henry the Eighth*, that contemporary coronation dress was worn. We have further evidence of Garrick's practice in Hayman's drawing for Charles Jennens' edition of 1770/4 (of which only five plays, including *Lear*, were published).[5] This drawing was almost certainly made within a few months of the Hayman frontispiece for Hanmer, for at the Folger Shakespeare Library there is a letter from Garrick to Hayman, written probably in the summer of 1745, giving precise indications of Garrick's reading of the scene, which Hayman followed exactly in his drawing (reproduced at Pl. II*b*, *Shakespeare Quarterly*, vol. IX, 2, Spring 1958).[6] Garrick writes:

If you intend to alter the scene in Lear [from the design used in Hanmer]...what think you of the following one. Suppose Lear mad, upon the ground, with Edgar by him; his attitude should be leaning upon one hand & pointing wildly towards the Heavens with the other. Kent & Footman attend him, & Gloster comes to him with a Torch; the real Madness of Lear, the frantick affection of Edgar, & the different looks of concern in the three other carracters, will have a fine effect.

The published drawing is a clearer indication of Garrick's intentions in the theatrical grouping than of costume and is of the greatest importance as an indication of the relations between artist and actor in the eighteenth century; but some costume details are of interest. Gloucester and Lear are roughly draped, though preserving that elegance in shoes and hose that we have found in earlier engravings; Edgar is naked to the waist, with his customary wisps of straw and his staff.

Peter van Bleeck's 'Mrs Cibber as Cordelia', painted in 1755 and now in the Memorial Theatre, Stratford-upon-Avon, gives us the heath scene as Nahum Tate rewrote it. Cordelia has returned from France and searches for her father on the heath until she and her maid, Arante, are attacked by 'two Ruffians' and rescued by Edgar, 'a wandering lunatic' (Pl. I*e*).

The brothers John and Alexander Runciman provide two most valuable complementary comments on the heath scene. John Runciman painted his 'King Lear in the Storm' (now in the National Gallery of Scotland, Edinburgh)[7] in 1767 and the costumes have many of the qualities common to the stage and to heroic painting at this period; Lear in full Van Dyck dress, regularly worn by characters of the pre-Tudor period, Kent in full Rembrandt costume, and the Fool, a young boy with little suggestion of professional motley. I am now inclined to identify the bearded man on Lear's right shoulder, in a turban, seemingly derived from a Rembrandt self-portrait, with Gloucester, and the figure to Kent's left with Edgar, though he seems rather fully clothed (Pl. I*f*). Alexander Runciman made a pen drawing of the same scene (Pl. I*g*),[8] a precise comment on the Shakespearian text at an identifiable moment, the entry of Gloucester with a torch, in a small, huddled group behind the main figures. The latter are all interesting in their independence of the stage and of contemporary critical comment. Edgar's rags and windswept blanket require no conventional addition of straw and staff from the stage representation; the Fool, with cap and bells but naked at the waist, has the most direct suggestion of this character's bawdy comments on Lear's predicament, unique, I believe, until the more indirect phallic suggestion in Robert Colquhoun's *décor* for the 1953 *King Lear* at Stratford-upon-Avon. Lear and Kent are conceived as a Passion group; both recall Dürer, Lear himself having a strong suggestion of a 'Man of Sorrows',[9] while the flying drape about his shoulders unites a frequent Renaissance form with a suggestion of a Scottish plaid, originally worn over the bare torso. The whole group is less ambitious than John Runciman's painting and carries the suggestion of an exercise in pastiche. Nevertheless by its many recollections of classical paintings and through them conveying scriptural overtones, it pursues interpretation of the scene well beyond the range of a conventional illustrator and of most theatre productions. The Runciman painting and drawing together constitute one of the highest points in visual comment in their century.

The Bell theatre editions and the plates for the British Library add little to our knowledge beyond confirming Garrick's pervasive influence over all productions of *Lear* in the latter half of the century. The drawing by Edwards, engraved by Hall for the 1773 Bell edition, illustrates unadventurously the caption, 'Thou art the thing itself'. De Loutherbourg's drawing for the 1785 edition shows Lear in a tattered ermine gown and an old and wizened Fool in a shapeless cloak. Burney's drawing, engraved by Hall in the same year, illustrates the caption, 'Ay every inch a king'; Lear is elaborately drawn, barefoot but with puffed hose, a doublet trimmed and a cloak lined with ermine, the whole engraving surmounted by the manifold emblematic suggestion of a pelican in her piety.

During the last decade of the eighteenth century and until the publication of Howard's edition by Cadell in 1832, there was a strongly classical tradition in setting and illustrating *Lear*. At its most individual this is seen in Fuseli's contributions to the Boydell Gallery and to the Rivington *Shakespeare* of 1805. The Boydell plate engraved by Richard Fenton illustrates the rejection of Cordelia in the first act; it has a characteristically febrile atmosphere, in strange contrast to the heavily draped, 'Gothic revival' hall. Lear and his courtiers have a suggestion, no more, of classically draped figures; Goneril and Regan are drawn with the elaborate head-dresses and closely-moulded, long-limbed draperies of Fuseli's courtesan figures, a manner scarcely modified when he depicts Cordelia and perpetuated in the scene from the last act, engraved by Cromek for the Rivington plate (reproduced here at Pl. II*a*). Two others of the Boydell paintings, by Benjamin West and James Barry, are in the grandly classical manner of the History paintings which the Boydells wished explicitly to foster. West's figures are all draped (even the unusually dignified and seated Edgar) and have little precision of form or period. Lear wears no regal costume, though the soft drapery of his toga-like outer garment appears flecked with a suggestion of ermine. Gloucester's torch throws a strong light on an augustly bearded and powerful Fool, in a belled hood with ass's ears. James Barry's painting is more precise in its historical suggestions. Dover is backed by a classical landscape under whose cypresses trilithons from Stonehenge are elongated to Grecian proportions and grace. Lear wears a furred gown but he is surrounded by soldiers and courtiers in an approximation to Roman costume (Pl. II b). A minor point of interest in these Boydell plates may be seen in Schiavonetti's engraving after Smirke, in which the Fool on the heath closely resembles the boy-fool in Runciman's painting, both in costume and bearing.

At this same period, in the last decade of the century, two frontispiece engravings appear to preserve at least some details of actual theatre scene and costume. Each shows Kent in the stocks: in the Bellamy and Robarts edition of 1790 Lear is in doublet and hose, with a cloak and feathered hat and leaning on a tall and elaborate staff; in 1798 Stothard repeated the scene for Edward Harding's edition; Lear is almost identically costumed, even to the tall staff, but the cloak is now more clearly fur-lined in a 'Tudor' fashion, perhaps recalling the Holbein portrait of Henry VIII but more probably illustrating an actual costume on the stage of Stothard's day.

At the height of this classical manner we should expect a Kemble production. Roach has an engraving which records the production at Drury Lane on 13 May 1801; Kemble as Lear wore a very simple gown; Mrs Siddons's dress was high-waisted with puffed and slashed sleeves, a Regency mode later given scholarly finality by Frank Howard's drawings, published in 1832/3 by Cadell, *The Spirit of the Plays of Shakespeare, Exhibited in a Series of Outline Plates*. Howard declares the principles by which he dated the play before embarking on the costume drawings:

The date assumed for the occurrences which form the plot of this celebrated tragedy, is after the Romans had been in Britain but before the arrival of the Saxons. The costume entails some disadvantages from want of variety and, in many instances, want of elegance; but it has been deemed right to complete the illustrations upon the principle laid down of strict antiquarian accuracy; and it is hoped that character will amply atone for casual inelegancies.

Two drawings offer marked contrast in approach: the characters on the heath are in rather undifferentiated dresses, the main interest being in the Fool's coxcomb and belled ass's ears. A later drawing shows Cordelia at her father's couch; here the furnishing, with delicate scroll-work, small amphorae and two-handled cups, shows all the fashionable conceptions of classical setting.

While these attitudes had been crystallizing out for some thirty years, other artists, the Stothards, Smirkes and Thurstons, had continued their pedestrian frontispiece illustrations. Two little works stand out from this uninspired mass. The fourth edition of Lamb's *Tales from Shakespeare*, published by Godwin in 1822 contains in the first volume a 'Lear and Fool' (Pl. IIc). It is a curious scene: Lear is garlanded, wears a plain gown and a single sandal and is accompanied by the Fool in *Commedia* costume. Yet the setting is a cliff above a stormy sea. It has been assumed that the engravings for this edition were minor work by Blake, similar to his two engravings after Fuseli for the Rivington edition in 1805 but Sir Geoffrey Keynes treats the drawings for Lamb's volumes as Mulready's. The second of these more notable *Lear* illustrations during the Romantic period is the small Blake in the Tate Gallery,[10] which shows the unusual scene, not in the Shakespearian text, but regularly seen on the stage, of Lear and Cordelia in prison.

The first half of the nineteenth century saw two traditions in illustrating *Lear*, not always closely related: the acting.tradition, largely perpetuated by Edmund Kean, Macready, Samuel Phelps and Charles Kean; and book illustration, characteristically seen in the work of John Gilbert, in Knight's *Pictorial Shakspere* and in the Cowden Clarke volumes.

Macready first played Lear in London in 1834 and seems to have worked on the costume himself. He writes in his Diary: 'May 6. decided on Lear's dress, etc. Looked through prints for a head but found none affording more information than I already possessed', which appears to suggest that he was more interested in his make-up than in the costume for the part.[11] His diary for 10 January 1838 shows that he was pursuing the matter for his second and better-

Fig. 1. The costumes for Macready's production of *Lear* at Covent Garden in 1838.

known production, in which Shakespeare's text was to be restored: 'Called at the Garrick Club to look at some costumes for Lear; Saw Thackeray, who promised to send me a book on the subject.' This production is well documented from notices, plates and drawings: Fig. 1, part of a drawing from George Scharf's *Recollections of the Scenic Effects of Covent Garden Theatre, 1838–9,* shows Edgar's costume surviving unchanged from the previous century; Lear wears a simple gown edged with ermine, and the Fool, played by Priscilla Horton, wears a simply formalized coxcomb and a smocked dress edged with a child's nursery frieze of animals.

Samuel Phelps produced *Lear* in 1845; it has become customary to qualify any production of his with some such phrase as 'by the scholarly Phelps', and with justice. The evidence shows a gravity and breadth of approach to Shakespeare which contrasted healthily with the growing flamboyance of the other players. The Forrest Collection in the Birmingham Public Library contains a splendid colour lithograph published in Berlin,[12] which shows Phelps as Lear, wearing an enveloping blue cloak lined with fur, over a simple red gown, panelled and orffreyed in a gold and white chequer design. His costume accords with the general impression of unostentatious dignity in his productions.

Charles Kean's *Lear* was produced in April 1858 and became the mid-century focus of an argument over the propriety of 'Scenic illustration'. The *Illustrated London News* notice for 24 April is concerned about Kean's general approach: 'There is always a danger in scenic illustration pictorially carried out and archaeologically conducted, that the spectacular will overlay the dramatic', and though the critic is reassuring ('the subordination of the mechanist and painter to the poet and actor is duly maintained throughout'), the production seems to have been excessively elaborate.[13] The costumes seem to have been more modest than the settings, though the Fool wore a motley collection from several traditions: a cap with bells, a striped tunic and a diaper-checked pair of pantaloons.

The prolific book illustrations of this period show the same elaborate tendencies as the theatre but with more precision of detail. Knight's *Pictorial Shakspere* (1830–43) must suffice as representative of this abundance. This edition is usually pedantically 'accurate' but takes a sensible critical line over *Lear*, disavowing Douce (by implication, in one note, 'a professional detector of anachronisms') who had spoken of Shakespeare's 'plentiful crop of blunders' in this play. The editor is content to regard the play as 'describing events of a purely fabulous character' in 'an age to which we cannot attach a precise notion of costume (we use the word in its large sense)'.[14] For these reasons he does not object to seeing Lear painted with a 'diadem on his head, and the knights in armour', as in Harvey's frontispiece to the play in this edition.[15]

The years immediately following Knight's *Shakspere* saw an important development in historical sense, differing greatly from the 'modern dress' tradition of the eighteenth century and the growing archaeological precision of the nineteenth. In 1844, when Delacroix produced some of his finest lithographs of *Hamlet*, Ford Madox Brown was in Paris; in his exhibition catalogue of 1865 Ford Madox Brown describes his 'Lear and Cordelia', painted in 1848 under the influence of Delacroix:

Shakespeare's King Lear is Roman-pagan-British nominally; mediaeval by external customs and habits, and again, in a marked degree, savage and remote by the moral side. With fair excuse it might be treated in Roman-British costume, but then clashing with the mediaeval institutions and habits introduced; or as purely mediaeval. But I have rather chosen to be in harmony with the mental characteristics of Shakespeare's work and have therefore adopted the costume prevalent in Europe about the sixth century, when paganism was still rife, and deeds were at their darkest. The piece of Bayeux tapestry introduced behind King Lear is strictly an anachronism but the costume applies in this instance.

Madox Brown has here seen the ambiguities which Shakespeare introduces into any historical presentation and particularly into *Lear*. 'Roman-British' carries with it the implications of decayed grandeur and authority, a civilization poised between empire and barbarity. Most of the artists who have concerned themselves with scenery have been content with a rough magnificence in the interiors and an evocation of Stonehenge in exterior setting. But costumes set a further problem, hitherto not wholly faced, though Madox Brown has set out its terms. Shakespeare implies a remote period, latent in the characters and their mode of thought, while 'The Vines of France, and Milke of Burgundie' argue a later polity of Europe; the Fool and Edmund introduce still later overtones of courtliness, the Tudor court fools and their antecedents, and, in Edmund, the 'machiavel', still nearer Shakespeare's own day. Madox Brown's confident phrase, 'strictly an anachronism but the costume applies in this instance' justifies the still more far-reaching confidence of his claim, 'I have rather chosen to be in harmony with the mental characteristics of Shakespeare's work'; Cordelia's elaborate gown with the *fleurs de lis* of France preserves this temper, in the portion of his painting here reproduced at Pl. II*d*.

When, in November 1892, Irving produced *King Lear* at the Lyceum, he wrote in the preface to his acting version: 'As the period of King Lear, I have chosen, at the suggestion of Mr Ford Madox Brown...a time shortly after the departure of the Romans, when the Britons would naturally inhabit the towns left vacant.' The Black and White Souvenir of the production, illustrated by Bernard Partridge and Hawes Craven, shows Irving to have employed his usual team of designers, Hawes Craven and Harker, but the 'Synopsis of Scenery' carries the note: '*The Scenes of Lear's Palace and Gloster's and Albany's Castles are from designs by* Ford Madox Brown' (Irving says specifically that Madox Brown 'designed three scenes in the first and second acts'). Examination of the plates in the Souvenir shows that the 'Tent in the French Camp' owes nothing to Madox Brown's painting, either in temper or design, and any creative ambiguity in the period suggested has been removed. A short way has been taken with any 'anachronism' in costume. Courtiers are dressed with a suggestion of Roman armour but the helmets are frequently horned in the 'Saxon' manner. The women are elaborately gowned with a vague suggestion of early mediaeval detail in girdles, fillets, flowing head-dresses and pieces of jewellery. The Fool wears a conventional court jester's dress but his sandals have extended thongs carried over the calves, appearing to have been but recently promoted from villeinage. Lear's costume, 'of barbaric splendour', may be seen in Partridge's drawing from the Souvenir (Pl. II*e*).

Irving's production established the main lines of elaborate spectacle and of dating the play until almost our own day. Designs for *Lear* since the late war sufficiently demonstrate contemporary eclecticism in *décor* and costume. In 1946 Roger Furse designed the Old Vic *Lear* for Sir Laurence Olivier and all the costume drawings echo the colours, patterns and designs of figures in the Winchester Bible. The 'Byzantine' distortion of curve and proportion in these drawings, imposing a suggestive Christian allusion upon the pagan setting, was a tentative return to the complexity of Madox Brown's approach. A wholly different ambiguity, justified as an isolated experiment, was found in the Stratford *Lear*, designed by Isamu Noguchi and produced by George Devine in 1956. Here the setting and costumes transferred the tragedy to an alien medium, an approximation to the conditions of the classical Japanese stage, and imposed upon the production a fundamentally different sophistication and conventionality. The producer and designer, with Sir John Gielgud who played Lear, published a brief statement in the programme:

Our object in this production has been to find a setting and costumes which would be free of historical or decorative associations, so that the timeless, universal and mythical quality of the story may be clear. We have tried to present the places and characters in a very simple and basic manner, for the play to come to life through the words and acting.

The production released interpretation from any banality but it was by its nature unrepeatable. Two previous productions in this country within this decade had brought to bear the individual vision of creative artists on the problems considered here: Leslie Hurry's designs in 1950 and Robert Colquhoun's in 1953. Hurry, with some of the most intense insights into Shakespeare's tragedies in our day, employed a less macabre range of images than those which had distinguished the two productions of *Hamlet*—play and ballet—for Robert Helpmann. Colquhoun's designs in 1953, when again the play was produced by Devine, made no attempt to particularize period, so that ambiguities based on deliberate anachronism were set aside. The costumes, however (Lear and the Fool are illustrated at Pl. II*g*), were heavy, even ponderous in impression, with leather and much quilting, and were congruous with the simple, monumental sets. Though the costumes were richly varied, they were in a small range of hues and a limited number of tones, but unity was kept by the motifs or bands of white introduced at some focal point in each costume. It was noteworthy that the Fool's obscenities in the heath scenes were now visually suggested not in costume but in the set itself.

Lamb, in common with other Romantic critics, had considered *Lear* too vast for adequate stage presentation; it is scarcely necessary to say here that there are imponderables in the play which defy theatrical production or indeed any other visual interpretation—and in this *Lear* is not unique. Yet there is no major play of Shakespeare's that has more successfully and in more varied fashion challenged the creative comment of painters, engravers and artists in theatre *décor*. Each comment is partial and inadequate, reflecting some of the distortions as well as the critical insights of their age, but they have their cumulative power and penetration, contributing another dimension to the criticism of Shakespeare's text.

NOTES

1. Leslie Hotson, *Shakespeare's Motley* (1952).
2. Hotson, *op. cit.* pp. 5 n., and 38.
3. See *Shakespeare Quarterly*, vol. IX, 2 (Spring 1958), W. M. Merchant, 'Francis Hayman's Illustrations of Shakespeare', where the Hanmer edition in the Folger Shakespeare Library, Washington, containing Hayman's own drawings bound in with Gravelot's engravings, is discussed; eight plates are reproduced.
4. Ellis Waterhouse, *Painting in Britain* (1953), pp. 228–9, suggests that Zoffany may have had a hand in Wilson's painting.
5. A. C. Sprague, *Shakespearian Players and Performances* (1953), p. 34.
6. This plate is reproduced with the Hayman drawings in *Shakespeare Quarterly*, IX, 2, 1958 (note 3 above). In the same issue of the *Quarterly* Kalman Burnim considers 'The Significance of Garrick's Letters to Hayman' and quotes in full the letter cited here.
7. This plate has been treated at length in Merchant, *Shakespeare and the Artist* (1959), chapter XII.
8. National Gallery of Scotland, Edinburgh, D. 313. I owe knowledge of this drawing to the kindness of Keith Andrews, Keeper of Prints and Drawings at the National Gallery of Scotland.
9. Mrs Eric Newton, to whom I put this suggestion, amplifies it by referring the Lear head to Tietze, *Dürer Cat.* I, 183, and suggests further that Kent recalls a Dürer drawing in the British Museum, Tietze, I, 226.
10. Reproduced in Merchant, *op. cit.* Pl. 29 *b*.
11. Macready would have found many Heads of Lear in the drawing portfolios of the preceding half-century. Reynolds has a noble drawing and there is a very fine Romney drawing in the Folger Library. Nearer his own day, Sir John Gilbert made one of his best drawings of Lear for Staunton's *Shakespeare*.
12. The lithograph, in Forrest, *King Lear*, II, 531, is headed, 'Friedrich-Wilhelmstädtisches-Theater' and published by Eduard Bloch.
13. The Victoria and Albert Museum has a full series of designs for this production; the design by Grieve for the heath scene is reproduced in Merchant, *op. cit.* Pl. 71 *c*.
14. Presumably by 'costume' the critic here means *décor* 'in its large sense'.
15. The set of Knight's *Pictorial Shakspere* in the Library of the University College, Cardiff, contains Harvey's drawings bound in with the engravings. The frontispiece for *Lear* has, in Harvey's drawing, only a slight suggestion of Roman costume which is clarified in the engraving.